PURPOSE, PASSION, AND COLLEGE

PURPOSE, PASSION, AND COLLEGE

How To Choose The Right College, Major, And Dream Career!

Dennis Stemmle

College Success Academy
COLLEGE SMARTER NOT HARDER

Purpose, Passion, and College

How to choose the right college, major, and dream career!

ISBN-13: 978-1-7354030-6-9 (Paperback)

BONUS OFFER!

Thank you so much for purchasing your copy of Purpose, Passion, and College. If you are anything like me, you are much more of a visual/auditory learner.

With that in mind, I have recorded a series of deep dive training videos that walks you through the key elements/components of the book. These videos are designed to help you get the most out of this book. To access the videos, please go to:

SCAN ME

www.PurposePassionAndCollege.com

Acknowledgments

It is through others that I have gained the knowledge and experience that so powerfully contributed to me becoming the person I am today. I am eternally grateful for these mentors, coaches, and friends.

This shared knowledge provided a foundation for any success I have been fortunate enough to achieve.

To all the college students that provided feedback and insights on this project, I am grateful for the time you took to make this book better.

To my son Bradley who strongly encouraged me to share my thoughts and ideas with college students everywhere.

To my wife Karen, whose support has been endless.

Finally, a thank you to the young men and women I have taught over the years. May you always choose to pursue your purpose and be the best version of yourself!

Table Of Contents

Introduction!

"Every new beginning comes from some other beginning's end." — Seneca.

For most young adults, what college to attend or even if you should attend college is your first major decision. Our parents decided what town we lived in, what neighborhood we would grow up in, and what high school we attended, and so on. But as high school graduation approaches, young adults must face the challenging decision about how they are going to spend the coming years. While your initial choice does not necessarily confirm the exact course your life will take, it will be a starting point for your future adult life. Some students will choose to get started with their careers, others may take a gap year and take time off to travel, and many will get started pursuing higher education.

Going to college is a significant step. You are likely excited, nervous, and maybe even a little scared to start your life of independence away from the watchful eyes of your family, teachers, coaches, and other well-meaning so-called adults. Like many young people, you want to make new friends, earn your college degree, launch that dream career, and live happily ever after.

But like many, you might be feeling overwhelmed with all the seemingly endless choices that lay ahead. And some of you reading this book might already be a year or two into your journey, and you have come to realize the path you're on is no longer the path you want to stay on. You certainly would not be the first student to feel that way.

You might be shocked to learn that in the United States, we have the lowest college completion rate in the developed world! And shockingly, thirty percent of college freshmen drop out after their first year! 30%! And only around half of the students who enroll in college end up graduating with their bachelor's degree!

College is taking longer and longer to get through, with less than 60 percent of students who enter a four-year school actually finishing within six years.

The National Student Clearinghouse data shows that about one-third of college students transfer schools before graduating. And while the number of students that transfer varies greatly by college, the range typically falls between 15% and 40% of initially enrolled students. In fact, more than a third of college students transfer, and nearly half of those do it more than once.

Students transfer colleges for a whole host of reasons. Some students decide to transfer schools before making it to campus for their first class, while others, after spending a year or two at a college, are ready for a new challenge. In a large number of cases, the decision to transfer is driven by unforeseen circumstances or life events. And some students plan to transfer from the very beginning by enrolling in a community college or bridge program.

The Association of American Colleges & Universities data shows that transfers from community colleges represent around 15% of new enrollments at four-year institutions. While it certainly is not surprising that many students choose to transfer from their community college to a four-year program, it is a bit surprising how few students actually earn their four-year degrees. Columbia University's Community College Research Center data show that about 80% of students attending community college said they wanted to earn a bachelor's degree or higher. The shocking reality is that only about 30% made the transfer to a four-year school within six years of their community college enrollment.

Too many students choose a college for the wrong reason, then they choose a major for another wrong reason. Next, they choose their first job for the wrong reason, and one day they wake up and find themselves wondering how they got where they are.

So much of our education is skill-centered. We teach accounting, finance, marketing, history, art, economics, and so on. Students are expected to take these skills and figure out some way to use these newly acquired skills to build a rewarding career and life. However, we spent little to no time focused on teaching students how to identify the life they want and then how to acquire the skills and frameworks they need to start on the journey to creating a fulfilling life.

The Gallup organization consistently reports that nearly 70 percent of employees are actively disengaged. And The Conference Board reports that 53 percent of Americans are currently unhappy at work. Consider that for a second. Over seventy percent of the workforce is disengaged and unhappy in the work they do each and every day. That is an incredibly sad statistic.

Do we really believe our seventeen-year-old self is well equipped to determine what kind of work we want to be doing for the rest of our lives? Of course not! Is it realistic to believe you should know your purpose as a young adult? Of course not! In order for most of us to discuss our purpose, we have to first experience a lot. We need to embrace the process of finding our purpose and embarking on a journey of discovery that brings us joy, happiness, and fulfillment along the way. The alternative is just too costly!

How would you like to spend years in college and tens of thousands of dollars just to land a job that will ultimately make you unhappy? The system is broken for the vast majority of people, but you can do something about it. You can be in the small percentage of people who have engaging and fulfilling careers and lives. That is why I am so glad you have invested your time and money in this book.

As a college success expert, best-selling author, and university professor, I have had the opportunity to work with and impact thousands of students from all over the globe. And while my first three books focused on the skills and tools needed to achieve success in college, more and more students were telling me they felt like they were lost, that they were winning a game they were not even wanting to play. They were going through the motions hoping they would find their purpose and passion in college, but they were feeling more lost than ever. They were frustrated, stressed, and felt like they were falling behind their peers, who seemed to have it all figured out.

I realized so many students were working hard to optimize the wrong equation. They were on the fast track but not the right track. They needed a guide to help them find their purpose, their passion, and ultimately their dream career. The book you are now reading is my effort to help you start on the right path. It serves as a compass and framework to guide you on your journey of discovery.

This book is different than any of the other books out there on how to choose a college, a major, and a career. This book does not start with that end. It starts with self-thought, reflection, and personal discovery. Because here is the reality, you won't be able to effectively understand how to pick a college, a major, or a career until you understand how those decisions fit into the rest of your life.

Once we have a framework and compass for discovering our life's purpose, we can then effectively choose a college, major, and career that will be fulfilling. Please don't skip the exercises and worksheets in this book. Without deep reflection, we can't properly view our college and career choices through the proper lens. Life is simply the compound effect of the choices we make. As such, it is critical we make our choices through the lens of our life's purpose.

In order for the process to work, you must begin with some serious self-reflection. Many students are tempted not to assess their lives because they think it is uncomfortable, silly, or even a waste of time. If you are feeling any of that, just realize you are encountering a belief. I encourage you to set that belief aside for a short period of time. After all, when you're done with this book, you can always revert back to that belief, but I know you won't want to. The truth is, this is where you will put everything you learn into action. This is the process that will allow you to create the life of your dreams. Trust the process!

A word of caution. There is no single optimal path for you in your life. There are actually many paths you could go down and create an amazingly happy and fulfilling life for yourself.

E.E. Cummings, Poet (1894-1962), said that "the hardest challenge is to be yourself in a world where everyone is trying to make you somebody else." I believe in today's modern world, it may even be more difficult to first determine what it even means to be yourself.

You are not going to know what you actually want until you first figure out what you might want and what you don't want. The idea is to generate a lot of ideas and possibilities without passing judgment on those possibilities. Think of yourself as an explorer on an adventure, a mission to discover new lands. You are in discovery mode, not judgment mode. There will be plenty of time for judging later. Life is best lived abstractly, not painted by numbers.

Give yourself the time and permission to try many things and embrace the journey of self-discovery and resist the cultural push to embrace society's blueprint for your life. Pursuing your purpose is a dynamic activity, not a one-time thing. Finding your purpose is a lifelong pursuit. We likely will find many different purposes to pursue as we gain more life experiences and mature. With all that said, let's jump in.

What is a Purpose, And Do You Need One?

"The purpose of life is to live it, to taste experience to the utmost, to reach out eagerly and without fear for newer and richer experience." – Eleanor Roosevelt.

Have you ever asked the question, "Why are you here?" "What am I meant to do with my life?" Or, more directly, "What is my purpose in life?"

When I talk to students and ask them what they want from their lives, the vast majority say they just want to be happy, be successful. But when I ask them how they plan to do that, well, most admit to having no idea. When I ask them what success and happiness actually look like, they are typically vague. When pressed, they typically will say they want a good-paying job, a great spouse, and a happy family. As college students, their immediate focus typically is on graduating and finding a career that will set them on their way.

I often joke that in college, we are charging students tens of thousands of dollars a year so that eighty percent of them will be unhappy and disengaged in their careers. You won't see that knowledge bomb on any university websites. But it really doesn't have to be that way for you.

Imagine that you are so focused on your purpose that you jump out of bed each day, energized to start your day. Imagine feeling fulfilled and grateful every night for the contributions you made and the experiences you had. This really can be your life. I know it's true because I live that life daily, and millions of others around the world do as well.

The reality is that most people don't live their dreams and don't magically realize their purpose for being. A significant amount of the population goes through life spending countless hours searching, dreaming, and wondering what their purpose is. Most will never find their purpose. Some people will find themselves searching their entire life for their purpose, but most will stop very early in their lives. The vast majority of people (83%) are like leaves blowing in the wind. They have no goals. And the small percentage of people who do set goals, research has shown that only 8% of those individuals are successful in achieving their goals. The harsh reality is that most people will not do the work required to discover their talents, passions, and purpose. They expect it to magically appear like a pot of gold at the end of a rainbow.

Only one in four individuals report having a sense of purpose in their lives. In my experience, that number is likely closer to one in ten. Most of us devote a considerable amount of our life to our work. The average person spends over 90,000 hours on the job throughout their life. With all that time working, it just makes sense to want to be doing something that fulfills your purpose.

Look at the below information about the importance of having a purposeful work-life:

- More than 9 out of 10 workers would take a 23% pay cut if they had the opportunity to do purposeful work.
- Meaning is the new money. A significant number of studies have shown employees want their work to be meaningful.
- 80% of employees would prefer to have a supervisor who cared about meaningful work and success in work than receive a 20% pay increase.
- Those who have meaningful work emerge as leaders and top contributors.
- Turnover rates are lower when work is meaningful.
- Employees with meaningful work are happier, more productive, and harder workers.

Finding your purpose is a lifelong pursuit. We typically will find many different purposes to pursue as we gain more life experiences and mature. Of course, there are the lucky few, the ones who discover their purpose early on, but for most people, their purpose becomes clear over time. It is the active pursuit, the journey of discovery, that energizes us. The process of actively figuring out exactly what you were meant to do on this earth evolves and changes. As you gain more life experiences and more vantage points, your purpose will grow to reflect your growth.

Let's look at a quick example of how this all can play out when choosing a college, major, and career. Maybe you love doing something, what that might be is not important, but you think you will never be able to make a living at it.

But here is the rub, there is likely a path to turn that enjoyment into a career. Let's look at just one example. For the purpose of this example, let's say you love to paint and you love art history. But you also realize your talent is not on par with the great masters, and last time you checked, there were not a lot of art history majors killing it financially. So, you quickly dismiss the idea of an art-related career and start looking for a major that will make you a good living.

But what if you thought about the idea differently. You use what is called a mind map (I will show you how to do this exercise later), and after doing this exercise, you discover you could create a business that takes groups of people on tours to different museums, and they can learn about art and culture. Further, you realize these types of clients also are interested in architecture and history, so you add walking tours of the city with its deep culture and history to your business. Art is your passion and your purpose, and it matters to many other people as well. You thus create a thriving business that would allow you to share this passion with people every day.

But how does all this help me choose a college and a major? I am glad you asked! Armed with all this knowledge, you now choose to narrow down your college shortlist to schools in cities rich in culture, with world-class museums and lots of tourists who visit each year. You could also decide to look at a college that would not only allow you to pursue a major in art history on that shortlist but also would allow you to minor in business or, at a minimum, offer some business courses. Maybe you look at universities with well-established internship programs with museums. The point is that you are now focused on choosing a school that will accelerate your purpose, not on some other reason like just getting away from home or getting away from the cold winters.

Traditional college selection advice rarely gets you to the best answer. The so-called experts would have you focus on things like the academic ranking, the size of the schools, the competitiveness, etc., and all these are important, of course. But without a deep understanding of your purpose, passion, and talents, you are optimizing your college selection for the wrong things. No wonder a full third of students transfer colleges before graduating!

Discovering your purpose is the initial phase in creating a fulfilling life. It allows you to do work that fills you with passion and leverages your talents to make this world a better place. We need to understand just what purpose is and why it's so important to you. Setting goals and making life choices without understanding your purpose, passions, and talents is like cooking a great meal with all the right ingredients in all the right proportions, but you prepared a great meal with food you simply don't like to eat. You achieved your goal, but it left a bad taste in your mouth.

What is Purpose

It was Oliver Wendell Homes who wrote, "Destiny is not a matter of chance; it is a matter of choice." To fulfill our ultimate destiny in life, we must first get clear on our purpose.

"Everyone has a purpose in life, a unique gift or special talent to give to others. And when we blend this unique talent with service to others, we experience the ecstasy and exultation of our own spirit, which is the ultimate goal of goals." – Deepak Chopra.

If we look up the word purpose in the dictionary, we find the following: **"Purpose (noun) is the reason something is done, created, or exists."** When many people reflect on their purpose, they find themselves driven by a "Why." We wonder why someone was driven to pursue what they are working on. We may ask ourselves why a particular task or job matters. We want to pursue work that is meaningful.

"Unless we stand for something, we shall fall for anything." – Rev. Peter Marshall.

The need to connect and serve others so you can feel more fulfilled motivates people to fulfill their own goals and help develop their sense of purpose. Your own life purpose will be your north star, driving you to get up each day in pursuit of the things that matter the most to you. Purpose is truly a motivating force and provides the fuel you need to achieve your life's goals.

Your purpose can serve more than just your motivation. Your purpose can be the lens you use when making decisions. It can drive your behavior, frame your goals, and gives you a clear sense of direction in your life.

For some, purpose is driven by the work they do. Others may be driven by their relationships with their family and friends. Others may be driven by their spirituality or religious beliefs. While others are driven by creating what they view as a well-balanced life and finding their purpose in key areas of their life. Underlying these desires are what I call the big five blocks of life: finances, health, relationships, career, and personal life.

Purpose will be unique to each individual. The path you choose will be different from the path someone else chooses. And while you certainly will build your future on the shoulders of those who went before you, as the Greek philosopher Heraclitus said, you can't step in the same river twice. Things are constantly changing and thus are never exactly the same.

Your purpose will likely change throughout your life as you grow and gain more life experiences. As you are finding yourself, growing, and evaluating what you are doing with your life, you can use the following questions to help you recalibrate your purpose.

- What are my core values?
- Who do I admire and why?
- What music, books, movies, or trends get me excited?
- What would you do if you won the lottery?
- When do you feel the most fulfilled?
- What is my purpose in life?

Your purpose is your reason why. It's the driving force behind your actions, your goals, and your fulfillment in life. Living a life of purpose, either through your studies, work, volunteerism, or some other way, helps you become fulfilled and happier.

Why You Need A Purpose

"If the ladder is not leaning against the right wall,
every step we take just gets us to the wrong place faster."
– Stephen Covey.

We have looked at what purpose is. But why do you need a purpose? Why can't you just set some goals and focus on once achieving them? Why can't you just keep doing the things you always have done? There are 5 core reasons why you should have a life purpose.

1. **Purpose is where you start living your best life**. It's the initial step to living a more mindful life. Without a clear sense of purpose, you might find yourself pursuing goals for months or even years only to realize you did not actually want what you achieved. When you are clear on your purpose, you understand what you want to accomplish. But you also understand the why behind why you want to accomplish it. With this knowledge, you can align your goals and take the right actions each day, so you are creating a life of meaning. With a clear purpose, you can set the right goals with aligned actions and plans.

2. **Purpose brings clarity to what is actually important**. Purpose becomes the lens that allows you to understand what is important to you and what isn't. Most people stay busy being busy. They get caught up in things that don't make a real impact in creating the life they really want. They get focused on the disease of more. They want more money, more impressive houses, cars, and other material possessions. With purpose in life, you can direct your energy and focus on what is truly important to you.

3. **Purpose creates meaning in your life**. Your life gains tremendous clarity and direction. You find the motivation to not waste time in a job and other activities that don't serve your purpose. When your career is aligned with your life purpose, you find yourself working with others who share your vision. Identifying your purpose starts you down the path of transitioning to your ideal life and becoming the best version of yourself. With clarity of purpose, you can go to work creating a long-term plan that will allow you to pursue that purpose.

4. **Following your purpose energizes you with passion**. This drive fills you with energy and excitement every day to be doing what you are, creating, and moving forward. When you aren't living a life without purpose, your days tend to drag on, and you are bored and frustrated. You find yourself living for weekends and dreading the alarm going off each Monday morning. There's no excitement about the work you are doing. You find yourself repeating the cycle over again each and every Monday morning.

5. **With purpose, you can live life on your terms**. Most people look at goals and success as an end to itself. But success is not an end; it's actually a journey. It's the effect of pursuing and completing the things that you love to do. It means living a life of alignment with your passions, goals, skills, and your purpose. When you pursue your passions, success is in the journey, not the end destination.

Instead of setting your sights on material success as the end, identify what you truly care about, your purpose, and then put all your energy and effort into making that purpose a reality. When you discover your purpose, you will naturally dedicate your life to pursuing it because it fulfills you, and you naturally get better at it because you devote time to learning, training, and acting on it.

There you have it. Five great reasons why you should have a life driven by purpose. Having a purpose keeps you excited about what you are doing and helps you stay focused on your goals and take the actions needed to achieve your purpose.

But wait… There's More

"The human race is a monotonous affair. Most people spend the greatest part of their time working in order to live, and what little freedom remains so fills them with fear that they seek out any and every means to be rid of it."
- Johann Wolfgang von Goethe

Do you really want to graduate college only to wake up each day dreading spending another day at a job you hate? Do you want to feel dissatisfied with your life? Of course not, but all too often, that is exactly what happens. In my experience, this happens because people haven't taken the time to determine what their purpose is in this life. It takes hard work to uncover what that purpose is, but it is within you.

When you live your life in alignment with your purpose, it allows you to fill your days with meaning and enjoyment. The advantages of knowing your life purpose are far-reaching. Students with a clear purpose report:

- Having more fun in their daily lives.
- Having a greater passion for life.
- Having a high level of motivation in pursuing their goals.
- Having a connection with something bigger than themselves.

Discovering your purpose in life will motivate you to change how you live. It will add meaning and focus to your every decision and action. It will guide you in your life choices and pursuits.

Reveal Your Purpose

It takes a great deal of self-reflection to identify your purpose. To discover your purpose, you have to ask yourself the right questions. You have to maintain an open mind and not filter yourself when answering questions. Answer these useful questions to help reveal your purpose:

1. How would you like to spend your time if you knew you only had ten more years to live? By establishing a hard deadline, we are much more likely to focus on the truly important things in our life. With a clear deadline at hand, we eliminate daily distractions. Write down all the ideas that come into your mind. Don't filter your thoughts. The things on your list are the things we want to dive deeper into. For each idea on your list, ask if you would like to spend your life engaged in this activity.

2. Another exercise is to future cast. Jump forward thirty years and ask yourself: How would I like to be remembered by those closest to me? This may include your spouse, children, friends, coworkers, etc. Spend some time thinking and reflecting on how you would like others to remember you. Once you understand how you would like to be remembered, draft a plan to live your life that way.

3. What did you enjoy doing when you were younger? What are the activities you spend hours doing as a younger you that you no longer do? As young children, we spend little time worrying about what others think, and we just do what we enjoy doing.

4. As we move closer to becoming teenagers social pressure kicks in. We develop a need to fit in and impress others. This need moves us away from the things we love to do. Sure, some activities we just outgrow, but adulthood finds us worried with the practicality of our choices.

5. What level of discomfort can you handle? Most tasks have an uncomfortable, boring, or unpleasant side at some point. Your life purpose will be no different. Are you willing to work long hours? Are you willing to take risks?

6. Think about the times when you have lost track of time. What were you doing? What were the topics, activities, or people involved? Compile a list of the things that had you so focused that you forgot about everything else going on.

7. What are the things you have always dreamed about? What are the things that would hold you back from pursuing your dreams? Fear? Money? Expectations? Knowledge? Confidence? Maybe somebody told you to get your head out of the clouds. Whatever the reason, identify those things that are holding you back.

8. What groups or communities could you serve? Develop a list of your passions, skills, and talents that you could use to benefit the world.

9. Who are the people that inspire you the most? What things about them inspire you? Could you integrate that inspiration into your own life in some way?

10. List your natural talents? What areas have you excelled at? Are complex ideas easy for you? Do you excel in social skills? Are you a good writer or storyteller? Are you good with numbers? Is your talent musical or artistic? Are you a compassionate person? You can learn to be good at just about anything, but if you have the natural ability already, use it as a foundation for your purpose.

11. If you were asked to teach a topic to others, what topic would you choose? It's not only more enjoyable to teach subjects you like, but the things you like are probably sources of your deeper knowledge. Looking at topics that you would teach to others make good candidates for areas to discover your life purpose.

12. What are the things you do that give you enjoyment? Create a list of the things that you do that you enjoy or that make you feel good.

13. What are the things people come to you for help with? People will ask for advice from those they believe have some form of expertise greater than their own.

14. Imagine yourself at 80 years old. Imagine sitting on your front porch and reflecting on your life. What memories do you

want to have? What do you want to have accomplished? What types of relationships would you have experienced? How can you make that happen now? Imagining yourself in the final years of your life gives you a good idea of how you want to have lived your life.

As you search for your purpose, digging deeper into your talents, skills, wants, and desires are key. It's difficult to know what your purpose is if you don't know how you can use what you have.

Money Is Not Purpose!

"At the end of the day, we're humans, and we struggle with existential issues like what's the meaning of life, and who am I? And those sorts of questions don't go away when you get a bunch of money." - Brad Klontz.

One of the greatest challenges most students face is getting over the false belief that making a lot of money is the path to the good life. After all, they are in college to get a degree that will lead to a career that they view will make them a lot of money. As such, they want to become an accountant, lawyer, marketer, manager, and so on.

They have things backward; they are focused on what things they want, not on who they want to become. First, focus on who you want to ultimately become. Next, do the things you need to do to become that person. And ultimately, you will have all the things you want. It is one of the great ironies of life.

Money is not an end; it is a tool. Ask yourself why do you want to make a lot of money? Is it for the freedom of time? Is it to have more control over your life choices? Is it to increase your feeling of security? Is it to provide more for your family? Is it to buy yachts and fancy cars? Here is the thing, money only solves money problems. What is left is all the other problems money can't solve.

A study by Princeton researchers Daniel Kahneman and Angus Deaton showed that people tended to feel happier with the more money they made, but only up to a point. That point was estimated to be about $75,000 yearly ($90,000 in today's dollars). After that, they found that happiness leveled off.

A more recent 2018 study at Purdue University using extensive data from the Gallup World Poll found that the equilibrium income point for individuals is about $95,000 for life satisfaction and between $60,000 to $75,000 for emotional well-being. **Surprisingly, when people earned more than $105,000, their happiness levels actually decreased**.

It is probably shocking to find out that research consistently reveals that money is not the path to happiness. If you want to be happier, you shouldn't focus on a high-paying job. From a happiness perspective, it's more important that your work provides a true sense of meaning and purpose.

You should focus on pursuing a career that is aligned with your purpose, your core values, and talents. For example, maybe you find that protecting the environment, helping people, or teaching other people is very rewarding to you.

It has been said a journey of a thousand miles begins with a single step. This quote doesn't only highlight the importance of taking that first step but the required progression of valuing the headway that is, the steps that are required and ultimately connect you to your goal, which is your destination. The world we live in over indexes actions and goals that drive perceived security and financial results. When I ask students what they want, the vast majority say they just want to be happy, yet the decisions they make tend to be financially driven, not fulfillment and happiness driven.

Oftentimes, we believe that it's only the results deemed important by society that matter and anything else is simply a waste of time or simply a pipe dream. However, we often lose our values and even have the tendency to lose ourselves, our beliefs, and our identity when all we concentrate on is getting the results society deems important.

A singular focus on the expectations placed on us by others has driven many to compromise their own dreams and leading to frustration, regrets, and a place where they feel empty and lost. When we fail to enjoy the journey, we can miss some of the best parts of our lives. I know more than a few students that were so focused on starting their careers that they missed out on significant parts of the college experience.

Life is about stages, phases, and processes. When people are overly focused on the outcome alone, they miss out massively on the value of the journey. Gary Vaynerchuk, a multimillionaire businessman and social media personality, has said that he wants to "redefine success" as being happy versus making a lot of money. "I have an uncomfortable number of friends who make $12 million a year and are unhappy," he says. I think that is awesome advice! Now is the time for you to start living the life you deserve to live!

The Case Against Passion

The problem with the people who will tell you that you should not follow your passion is that they are right, at least in some regard. They usually will tell you the world doesn't care about your passion. The world doesn't care if you want to be an artist, a musician, an athlete, a business owner, or anything else for that matter. The world wants its desires and needs to be met. And the fact is, these folks are correct. Where their argument breaks down is they assume passions and market needs are mutually exclusive. I assure you they are not. Sure, you might not be the next Picasso, but I bet you could learn to be a very good artist. You could teach art, you could help artists market their art, own an art gallery, or any other of the hundreds of jobs in the art industry.

Commitment Pledge

I,_____________________________, being of sound mind and body, do hereby pledge to commit to pursuing the best version of myself. I will demand the best of myself. I will not coast down the path of least resistance but instead will thrive to unleash the incredible potential that is lying inside me.

I do hereby commit to completing the exercise in this book. I will invest the time and energy today so that I can make a profound impact on my future and the world around me. I will use this book to move forward toward my goals, dreams, and purpose!

Signature of Commitment

____

Date___________________________

Exercise 1: What Is Important To You?

Below is a list of thirty common core values. From this list, I want you to select three that matter the most to you. If you have a value that is not on this list, that is fine; go ahead and list that value.

For each value you have selected, I want you to reflect and write in your journal about why that value is important to you.

Next, I want you to write about a time you demonstrated that value. Where were you? Who was there? What were the circumstances?

Finally, I want you to pick a person(s) you admire who most embodies each of the three core values you selected. This can be one person, two, or three different people. I want you to write down in your journal why you choose these individuals to represent the core value.

Achievement	Independence	Security
Community	Kindness	Self-control
Creativity	Relationships	Spirituality
Enjoyment	Reputation	Tradition
Expertise	Responsibility	Vitality
Integrity	Honesty	Courage
Happiness	Humility	Accountability
Curiosity	Fairness	Leadership
Loyalty	Compassion	Empathy
Gratitude	Wealth/Success	Discipline

Our values are built as a result of our experiences. Our experiences shape what matters most to us. Purpose in life is built on what matters most to us. As we think about our core values, we are taking the first step toward a life lived with purpose.

The Cards We Are Dealt

We all have to play the cards we are dealt in life. Some of us are born with a Royal or Straight flush, while others are born with a poor off-suit hand. One of the biggest challenges in our lives is learning to get the most out of the cards we are dealt. In Matthew Kelly's book, *The Rhythm of Life*, he writes: "Everything is a choice. This is life's greatest truth and its hardest lesson." While we can't choose the cards we are dealt in life, we can choose how we play them.

On the South Side of Chicago back in 1908, there lived a six-year-old boy with his widowed mother. Lack of money was a big issue, so this boy (we'll call him William) got a job selling newspapers. William quickly learned that all the older kids had already secured the best corners for selling papers. When William tried to sell his papers anywhere near these high-traffic corners, the older and bigger boys threatened him with beatings. But William had already purchased a bundle of papers to resell, and if he could not sell them, he'd be out of all his money. So, what do you think he did? What would you do if you were six and couldn't sell your papers on the prized corners?

You guessed it—he looked for a different location. Not a better corner; all the good corners were taken. Instead, he recalled a restaurant he and his mom had often walked past. The restaurant was named Hoelle's Restaurant, and it was always packed. For William, the thought of going inside on his own was more than a bit terrifying, as he'd never been in such a nice restaurant. While he was nervous and afraid, before he could talk himself out of it, he quickly walked inside and sold a paper to the very first table, and another at the second, and then yet another at the third. As he headed to the fourth table, Mr. Hoelle grabbed William and quickly escorted him out the front door.

So, what do you suppose William did? Do you think he gave up and went someplace else? Not a chance; he just waited patiently until Mr. Hoelle was no longer looking, and he headed back into the restaurant. At the fourth table, the customer was so amazed by William's moxie that he not only paid for the paper but also gave William an extra dime before Mr. Hoelle escorted William back out the door again.

Most six-year-olds would be satisfied with selling four papers and getting a tip. But not William. He walked right back in and started selling again. At this point, the entire restaurant was cheering for William. As Mr. Hoelle attempted to escort William back out the door, one of the customers said to let him be, which Mr. Hoelle did. About five minutes later, William had sold all of his papers.

The following night, William was back, and Mr. Hoelle was ready to kick him out of the restaurant once again. But just as quickly as Mr. Hoelle had escorted William out the door, William had entered again. Raising his hands with frustration up in the air, Mr. Hoelle said, "What's the use?" and let him sell his papers. Ultimately, the two became great friends.

So, who was William? William, it turns out, was Mr. W. Clement Stone. He would go on to turn a hundred-dollar investment into several billion dollars and donate nearly $275 million to charity over his lifetime.

To be successful, you certainly need a goal, but you also need the type of perseverance and persistence young W. Clement Stone exhibited as a frightened but determined six-year-old boy. Stone once stated, *"Regardless of what you are or what you have been, you can still become what you may want to be."*

And that's not the only thing we can learn from six-year-old William. His motivation was high because he and his mother needed the money. He'd already invested his pennies in buying the newspapers, and there was no refund for unsold papers.

William, no doubt, was afraid, but he had a big why. That Why allowed him to push through that fear before the fear paralyzed him.

He understood going back into the restaurant after being thrown out might embarrass him, but he did it anyway because he was determined to sell those papers. William knew that achieving the goal was more important than the risk of being embarrassed.

He had the motivation and the determination to succeed, but perhaps most importantly, he had an amazing thought process that allowed him to find a new outlet for paper sales—it was almost impossible for him to fail. How you think matters, which means that how you think when you decide to launch your future really matters!

When it comes to your life, a small vision will limit your potential, but a big vision will pull you toward more success than you believe possible. James Allen once said, *"You will become as small as your controlling desire, as great as your dominant aspiration."*

Your Big "Why"

William's big "why" was the simple need to help his mom put food on the table. You can start just about any career with a little creativity. But the first question you should be asking yourself is not what career to start but instead asking what you want to achieve in your life. Do you want freedom? Do you want fame? Financial success? Do you want to make a difference? By knowing what you want, you'll be much more likely to push through the fear and be successful in figuring out how to fulfill your purpose.

Let me give you an example: Let's say you are offered $100 to cross a 4-inch wide beam some 100 yards between two skyscrapers 1,000 feet in the air. If you are like me, your reaction would be a quick no, along with some additional adjectives not suitable for printing in this book. But let us change one variable—instead of $100, you need to cross the beam to save the single most important person in your life. In this case, your reaction is completely different, and you will suppress the fear, take the risk, and cross the beam. What changed? Your "why" changed. If your "why" is big enough, you can achieve amazing things with your life. Know your "why," as it will motivate you through the setbacks and challenges you will surely encounter.

What Are You Supposed To Be Doing?

I didn't ask you what you wanted to be doing. I asked what you are SUPPOSED to be doing? Are you supposed to be an "A" student? Are you supposed to take over the family business? Go to Mom or Dad's Alma Matta? Are you supposed to be a star athlete? A head cheerleader? Pageant queen? Doctor? Lawyer? Accountant? Housewife? Husband? Are you supposed to get a great job, get married, have three kids, and head over to Mom and Dad's place every Sunday for dinner? Are you the one that is supposed to break the cycle of poverty? Are you to be the first in your family to go to college? What are your expectations of yourself?

Inside all of us is a voice in our head that takes all the spoken and unspoken expectations placed on us. We form a vision of what is expected of us and the person we are supposed to become. We may never say it out loud, but it is there. We feel it with every big decision we make. It tugs on us like gravity, and it has a strong effect on how we live our lives.

Many students, not knowing what they want yet in life, default to the person whom they are supposed to be. After all, my mom, dad, coach, grandparents, etc., are all pretty smart; they know and love me. They just want the best for me. I don't want to let them down. Many times, students have a direction they want to go, they don't know the exact details, but they are being pulled in the direction of their interests. They can't yet verbalize a career path, so they once again default to whom they are supposed to be. Still, others know exactly what they want to do, but they can't escape the gravity of who they are supposed to be.

We are all programmed by our families, schools, communities, and even society. Some of us reject this programming, others accept it, but we are all influenced by it. My job is not to pass judgment on any of your programs but to make you think and reflect on this programming and the impact it has on the decisions you have made and will make throughout your life.

The first step is to actually think about and get clear on the programming we have been given by those around us. And that is exactly what exercise two is all about.

Exercise 2: The Programming We Are Given

Open up your journal or notepad and write down the names of everyone in your family and inner circle. We want to list the names of everyone that has been important to us. This would include family, friends, teachers, coaches, mentors, etc.

Under each name on your list, start writing what each individual wants you to do with your life.

Don't overthink it here. Just start writing what comes to mind. In some instances, you may not know exactly what they want, but you have a very good feeling about the overall direction. For instance, your list might look something like this:

Dad: Be wealthy and secure – a doctor or lawyer.

Mom: Be curious and adventurous – start your own business.

Grandma: Follow your passion for music.

Aunt: Go to college, get married, raise a family.

Friend: Move as far away from this town as possible and have fun in college.

If you are like most students, you will see a mixed message and many messages may be in direct conflict with each other. We have to understand what others want from us so we understand how they may be influencing what we may actually want from ourselves.

Those we care about want to protect us, keep us safe, and help us from experiencing pain. As such, they will tend to over-index on security and high probability financial outcomes. However, these wishes are rarely aligned with our dreams for our lives. Our dreams are who we are! Those around us have their own dreams for us. Very few of those around us have the stomach to watch you struggle as you search for your purpose. They will adopt the most practical path forward for you. What you really should be doing is work that matters to you.

Exercise 3: To Live The Impossible Dream

Frank Sinatra sang the words… "To dream the impossible dream. To fight the unbearable foe. To bear with unbearable sorrow." I have discovered that those words resonate with so many people living a life built on the foundation of other people's expectations placed on them.

We are going to create a vision board representing all the expectations that everyone in your family and inner circle has placed on you.

Your vision board will be a poster-sized visual representation of the life you are supposed to live. It will include pictures and words that represent the expectations others have put on you. Have some fun with this. Grab some old magazines your mom or dad have lying around the house, and head online to your favorite blogs or social media sites. Cut out or print pictures and words that reflect the expectations others have for you. Paste or tape them to your poster board, grouping those expectations on your poster board.

Once complete, take a good long look at your board. How do you feel about who you are supposed to be? Use your journal to record the feelings you are having. Which images stress you, frustrate you, anger you, make you happy, and so on. Keep your board handy. We will come back to it in exercise five.

Exercise 4: You Just One The Lottery!

Each semester I pass out index cards to my students. I tell them you just won the lottery, but this is a unique lottery. With this winning ticket, you get to earn 10% of the future earnings of any other student. The student can be anyone in your peer group (similar age) from your high school, your college, fraternity, sorority, etc. You must know this individual, and you can't select your friend who will sign that big NFL or NBA contract.

I have my students write down the name of the person they selected and three reasons (specific traits they possess) why they picked the individual they picked. Some students do this exercise quickly, while others really struggle to identify one individual.

Right now, I want you to do this exercise. Write the one person you would love to receive 10% of their future earnings and three reasons why you chose that person. Once you have finished this exercise, save your answer for a little bit later, we will come back to your answers in exercise six.

Exercise 5: My Dream Board

Grab your "supposed to be" vision board and flip it over. We are now going to create your personal dream board. On your board, we want to visually represent the things that make you happy, the things that place a smile on your face, and the things that represent your future dreams and desires. Don't self-regulate here; dream big!

How similar or different is your board from others' expectations? Take some time to reflect on the differences and similarities between the two boards. Reflect on how strong those expectations are weighing or tugging on you. In your journal, I want you to list the three to five biggest conflicts or misalignments between your board and your "supposed to be" board. On a scale of one to ten, with ten being a huge misalignment and 1 being a small misalignment, rank each conflict or misalignment. Our goal here is not to solve these misalignments. We are just wanting to identify them and bring them to the surface.

Vision boards are a really good way to bring clarity to your emotions, feelings, and expectations. They help us take things from abstract feelings to specifics we can take action on.

Purpose Keeps You Enjoying Life

"As the struggle for survival has subsided, the question has emerged: survival for what? Ever more people have the means to live, but no meaning to live for."
– Viktor E. Frankl

When you live a life with purpose, you have a certain peace that comes from the clarity of your driving purpose. You will not lose months or years aimlessly wandering through your life. Purpose fuels your drive and keeps you motivated to pursue your goals. When things get difficult, and they will, your purpose drives you to overcome the obstacles in your path. Purpose gives your life a deeper sense of meaning, brings you more joy, and gives a positive outlook on your future career and life.

People who are driven by a purpose in their life are happier in life than those who do not have a clear life purpose. The clarity their purpose gives them allows them to form daily goals and actions so they can achieve what they want in life.

There are lots of ways for you to discover your purpose. Let's look at the following suggestions which can help you on your journey:

- Ask questions that cause you to reflect deeply on things you enjoy and want.
- Journal about the things that little voice in your head dreams about.
- Inventory the times and things that, when doing, you seem to lose track of time.
- Look for the connections in the things that make you genuinely happy.

It takes work, time, and self-reflection to learn your inner self and subsequently find your life purpose. Get in the habit of asking yourself important, tough questions, and most importantly, start to listen to the answers.

Once you have good insights into the direction of your life purpose, the next step is to focus on how to take action on this new knowledge. Dreams and ideas are easy; it's the doing that creates the challenge.

What Is Your Purpose - Worksheet

Answer these questions to help you identify your purpose in multiple life stages.

As a young child, what did you feel your purpose for being here was? Why?

____

____

As a teenager, what did you think your purpose might be? Why?

____

____

Currently, what do you feel your life purpose is? Why?

____

____

Explain in detail 3 reasons you need a life purpose and the benefits you'll receive.

____

____

Benefit:

____

____

Benefit:

____

____

Benefit:

____

____

Questions to Reveal Your Purpose

What creative hobbies or activities have you participated in from your teen years to now?

____

____

What things would you like to be known for or accomplish?

____

____

What qualities or characteristics do you want others to associate with you most often?

____

____

What are the things you enjoy doing so much that you often lose track of time when doing them?

____

____

My Personal Notes

____

____

____

____

Why did I ask you to write down three reasons you selected who you selected in the lottery exercise? The reason I did this was to provide you with some insights into what characteristics or traits you believed led to financial success. By stepping outside of yourself and forcing yourself to think about the traits others had that would lead to success, I removed any personal self-regulation you naturally would impose on yourself.

Exercise 6: Balancing The Scale

In the table below, I want you to write the three core values you selected as the most important to you in exercise one and the three success traits you identified in the lottery ticket exercise.

Core Value	Lottery Trait

Take a look at your list and ask yourself how aligned the two columns are? For instance, did you pick a friend because they had a success trait of entrepreneurship, a high-risk reward career, yet you selected security as a core value? Maybe you listed creativity as a core value but selected a friend who was going to be a CPA.

We are not concerned with right or wrong answers here. The goal here is to look for our blind spots. When we go to college, we are often highly focused on the financial aspects of our future without regard for how that career really fits with our core values. This quick exercise will help you see how well-aligned your core values are with your own vision of what financial success looks like. The more alignment we can create between the two lists, the more likely it is we will find happiness in our work. Open up your journal and write the answers to the following questions.

1. How many of your friends would have picked you for their 10% lottery ticket?

2. What things would you have to do/change to get others in your peer group to pick you?
3. How would you grade yourself in the three lottery traits your friend possesses?
4. Do you feel any of your core values are in conflict with the lottery traits you listed?

This is such a powerful exercise because once we detach our own egos and filters from the success equation, we are more likely to identify the traits we believe are the key to financial success. With this knowledge and some serious self-reflection, we can identify the gaps we need to fill in order to move rapidly in the direction of our dreams.

Exploring Your Talents To Find Your Purpose

"The person born with a talent they are meant to use will find their greatest happiness in using it."
- Johann Wolfgang von Goethe

When it comes to finding your purpose, what your current talents are can be a glaring hint. Please don't filter yourself here. I often hear students say things like… I am great at art, but I can't make a living with that. Or I can sing well, but that's just for church. I can jump very high, but there is no way to make a living with that talent! Our goal is to identify areas of skill and talent, not identify skills and talents we think will lead to a lot of money.

Maybe you don't yet know what your true talents are. Maybe your talents are hidden deep inside you, and I have yet to discover them. In that case, how do you know if they may be a part of your purpose?

Reflecting on and exploring your talents, even those that you may have forgotten about or might be hidden, will help you on the path to finding your purpose in life. We all have talents we use throughout our lives. In many cases, our talents may be so easy for us to use that we don't even think about having them.

I am often asked if finding purpose is something that is deeper than simply using your talents? Of course, but using your talents and skills as a part of your life's purpose is the key to truly finding joy in your life. We find the greatest happiness at the point where our talents and passions intersect.

When you recognize your distinctive talents, you uncover insights into why you make certain choices, why you enjoy different activities, and why you are better at certain things. When you explore your talents, you can see your purpose more clearly.

Talent is the ability that allows you to do something well, while purpose is the reason why you do something. So, talent and purpose align to create a life driven by purpose.

There are various types of talents we all have. There are inherent talents and the acquired talents we develop. Inherent talent is those talents that you naturally have; you were just born with. Acquired talents are those talents that you have developed. Both, however, take practice to develop and optimize.

As Stephen King said, "*Talent is cheaper than table salt, but what separates the talented individual from the successful one is a lot of hard work.*"

Talent has a way of guiding you in the direction of your life purpose. Talent gives you insights into what your purpose might be. We all have talents we can monetize. The sad part is that the vast majority of people are held back by fear or the false belief that their talents can make them a living.

Sometimes we don't know what our talents are? How can you be expected to explore your talents and find your purpose when you feel like you have no real talents or passions?

In this book, I will show you how to find your passions and talents and align them with your true purpose. You'll also discover ways to discover your talents and how to use those talents to fulfill your purpose.

"For anyone trying to discern what to do with their life: Pay Attention to what you pay attention to. That's pretty much all the info you need."
– Amy Krouse Rosenthal

I want to make an important point here. Your talents, passions, and purpose will continue to grow as you do. This will result in your purpose growing and even completely changing as you mature. That is to be expected. As I review my purpose each year, I look at my purpose through the following two lenses:

1. Does it move me toward a better version of myself, one that requires me to grow?
2. Does it ultimately improve the outcomes of my life and the others I serve?

I assure you that you won't find the path to your purpose while staying inside your comfort zone. The best version of yourself will be found well beyond the safety and comfort of your current state. The prior two questions will serve as your North Star, a guiding light, keeping you on the path toward your true purpose.

Explore Your Talents

> *"Practice isn't the thing you do once you're good. It's the thing you do that makes you good."* – Malcolm Gladwell.

The 10,000-hour rule is a concept that asserts that with 10,000 hours of practice, most people can develop almost any skill. The original foundation for this assertion was a 1993 study of music students in Germany. The students had put in an estimated 10,000 hours of practice by 20 years old. This rule was later popularized in Malcolm Gladwell's book *Outliers*.

Whether 10,000 hours is the magic number or not is not what is important. What is important is to realize most of us can develop our talents to a level where we can do almost anything we want to do within reason, of course.

Most experts will recommend that if you want to be happy in life, you will need to discover and develop your talents to become successful in living your purpose. But what if you don't know exactly what your talents are? Or maybe you have unidentified talents you aren't utilizing. How do you tap into those to find your purpose? Here are some ideas to get you started.

1. I am not a big fan of personality tests before, say, 25-26 years of age. It's not that they are not accurate; they do a very good job. My problem is that when young adults take these tests, they tend to adopt and accept the result as gospel. They immediately label themselves as an INTJ or ENFJ or what have you, and that becomes who they are. These tests typically help you define existing patterns in your personality. The theory is that once you realize what category you are in, you'll understand where your strengths and weaknesses are in everyday life. I find these tests

tend to limit students' perspectives at the very time they should be expanding their perspectives. With that said, when administrated by a trained counselor, these tests can provide some valuable insights.

2. Ask the people who are the closest to you what they would say your best qualities are and where they think your biggest areas for improvement are. Your friends and family will be honest about your qualities if you approach them from a mentorship perspective. Ask them what superpowers you have or could have. Your superpower is your talent that is related to your passion. Superpowers are anything that lights you up.

3. Hearing the different perspectives of those close to you is enlightening, and if you hear a lot of the same feedback, that is a key indicator of your talent and strengths. Use their perspectives of your talents to self-reflect and identify where you can lean in and where you need more work.

4. What makes you feel in the zone? Do you have times when everything feels easy and smooth? When you have this sense of ease, this is your inner talent coming out, and you lose track of time. Notice when you feel lost in the moment. Create more opportunities to create this feeling. When you find yourself in the zone, you want to pay close attention as it can lead you to your purpose.

5. Ask your relatives what you loved to do as a child. Sometimes, we lose track of the things we spent our time doing as kids. Maybe you played outside, reenacted plays, played sports, drew art, played soccer, and constantly played video games. These things are likely things you still would enjoy.

6. Look at how you spend your money, aside from necessities. This shows you what you enjoy. Maybe your biggest expense over the past year has been the cross-fit membership you love. Or maybe the training programs you bought on starting a business. Where you spend your money can lead you on the path to discovering your purpose. For example, the fitness lover could become a personal trainer, coach, or gym owner, helping others maximize

their health. The lover of training programs could become a teacher or creator of online courses to help others start a business.

7. Keep track of your ideas and thoughts in a journal. Find a time each day when you can capture your thoughts by writing in a journal. Maintaining a consistent stream-of-consciousness writing is an effective way to gain insights into your interest, passions, and talents. Go back and read your journal writings after a couple of weeks. You'll probably notice many of your thoughts will circle back to one or two ideas or themes. These ideas or themes usually point you toward where your talents and passions are. Reflect deeply on the questions and answers in your writing. What do you feel is missing in your life? What are you longing for? What opportunities do you want to see unfold?

8. Who inspires you? Sometimes seeing the talents of others who inspire us makes us realize what we enjoy. Ask the others you admire to mentor you or give you advice about how to develop your talent. Recognizing talent in others may reveal opportunities and connections and helps you think about your own talents.

9. Look at what entertains you. What music, podcasts, videos, movies, or social media channel subscriptions excite you? The things we consume show what we value. Glance through your collections to highlight one resonating idea. What lights your fire? Is there some way you can use and develop this talent? How will you connect with others who enjoy the same or similar things?

10. Remember when you have made an impact. When did someone thank you? When were you able to help someone in some way. Notice what you are thanked for often. Do you help simplify difficult concepts for other students? Do people always ask your opinion on difficult situations? Are you a good listener? Do you easily motivate others to get things done? These may seem like small talents, but when you can use them to help people, you are well on your way to living your purpose.

Discovering your talent often surfaces from looking at what comes naturally to you, asking others what they see as your talents, and doing some soul-searching. But it also can come from developing your talents in pursuit of something that is meaningful to you.

Finding Your Purpose Through Journal Writing

"Tell me to what you pay attention, and I will tell you who you are." – Jose' Ortega y Gassett.

I know most students are not huge fans of writing. Many would prefer to talk things over with others or simply think about things in their own head. But writing things down is an extremely powerful tool for discovering your talents and your purpose. Your vantage points change when you can see and read the thoughts you put down on paper.

Writing out your thoughts and ideas will often provide clarity and ah-ha moments. Journaling or free writing allows you to connect deeper and creates a dialog with your subconscious mind. Journaling is certainly not a new idea, and it is not some new age hocus pocus as many may have you believe.

Not only do celebrities like Lady Gaga and Gwyneth Paltrow use journals, but many historical figures like Leonardo DaVinci and Thomas Alva Edison, and many others who became iconic innovators, artists, and creators used journals to help them organize their thoughts and ideas. Even athletes like Serena Williams and Curt Schilling used journaling.

To get started journaling, begin with a dedicated notebook or journal and a pen. Find a quiet place to write for thirty to sixty minutes or so. Don't use your computer. The act of writing by hand allows you to engage different parts of your brain and is much more effective for journaling. Make sure you do this at a time when you won't be interrupted. If you are, you will need to restart the process from the beginning.

We are going to start with a quick breathing exercise to help clear your mind. The first thing you will do is close your mouth and breath in through your nose for four seconds. Hold your breath for seven seconds. And finally, you exhale through your mouth for a count of eight. This completes one cycle. Repeat for three more cycles. This method of breathing is called 4-7-8 breathing. This exercise works great to help reduce stress, and it will help you clear your mind for sleep as well.

The reason we want to clear our minds is that part of the problem with finding your purpose is our constant thoughts racing through our minds. It's easy to limit yourself when you let preprogrammed ideas become a part of the answer. The answers are found in places you haven't looked, so keeping an open mind is necessary for this writing exercise.

Now it's time to start writing. On top of the page, write the question, "What is my life purpose?" This communicates and provides direction to your subconscious on the purpose of the writing. Start writing. Write whatever comes to mind. Write down everything. If you think to yourself, "This is a dumb idea," then write that down. The key is to not judge or restrict your thoughts.

During the first ten minutes or so, we are usually getting rid of the mental clutter still in our minds. Keep at the writing process. Eventually, you'll stall and want to quit or move on to something else but fight that urge and keep writing.

You won't find your life purpose in the first 60 minutes of journaling. But you need to stay with this activity daily until you discover your life purpose. How will you know when you hit on your life's purpose? You just will. It might fill you with excitement, fill you with a deep sense of calm, an emotional surge, or bring you a certain clarity in your mind. Just keep writing until you are certain.

Free writing and/or journaling gives you a chance to dig deep into what really matters to you. It helps you put aside your ego and any preconceived ideas of what you think or have been told your purpose is. So, give it a chance.

Most people that attempt this exercise will quit before reaching the end. Be one of the few that actually completes the process. Give it a chance. You have nothing to lose and a life of purpose to gain.

Exploring Your Talents

Understanding and exploring your talents is one of the tools you can use to help discover and refine your life's purpose. We can look at how you use your natural talents in your everyday life. Does it feel like you're using your talents in pursuit of your purpose, or does it feel like your talents are being locked inside you? If you don't feel like you are getting to use your talents, it's time to explore how you can use them to fulfill your purpose.

1. **Remember what excited you as a young child.** Remember your happiest memories from elementary school. What about those memories made them enjoyable? What were the common threads in each experience?

   For example, were you highly competitive as a 10-year-old? Maybe you loved running. You couldn't wait for recess every day so you could take on the other kids in a race. You lived for those times. Or maybe you were working on competitive, team-oriented projects where you had a knack for pushing the team's grade to the top of the class.

   When you think about your childhood memories, think about what types of activities you do as a young adult that offer the same thrill. You're probably still highly competitive, but now you're competing to win scholarships, Greek, or club positions. Or do you love difficult, strategic projects you do for your church or at work?

   Notice that what thrilled you in elementary school and what thrills you now are similar. You're still using your talent, just in a different theme. If you aren't utilizing what excites you in your major and everyday life, find ways you can incorporate that into your time at school with clubs and activities.

2. **You lose track of time when doing this**. Imagine it's late Saturday morning. You have no obligations, places to be, or things taking up your time. You have an empty calendar for a few hours of free time. It's your time to do what you want. You start doing your favorite activity. Maybe it's working out or playing

video games. Or you sit down to write the next great American novel. Or you could be developing a business plan for a side hustle you've been working on for months.

Whatever the activity, you are deeply focused on your thoughts, blocking out everything else. You lose track of time. Before you know it, it's late afternoon, and you haven't even had lunch.

Look at these moments closely. If you are so captivated by an activity that time is lost, you're in the flow of your purpose. These are moments you are likely utilizing the natural talents that you are meant to be using and sharing.

How can you use your talent to create a career and life that fulfills your purpose? Can you create video games that people love to play? How can you turn writing into your life's purpose? Can your side hustle grow into your main hustle?

3. **What do you yearn to do?** What desire do you have that needs to be fulfilled? Do you love to write? It's the perfect time in history to write a book or start a blog. Do you love to be on camera? Perfect. Create a YouTube channel and post some videos. Find products to promote via affiliate offers or develop your own offers. As your subscribers grow, you can earn advertising and sponsorship income.

   Do you love connecting with and meeting new people? Launch a meet-up on campus for students and locals in your area of interest. And if all this goes well, maybe you combine these activities into a monthly meet-up for other content creators and YouTubers.

4. **Take inventory of your talents**. What things do you have a natural aptitude for? Don't include things you're good at but don't enjoy doing. Notice the things you do that delight you. Maybe you don't do them often because you think you aren't good at them, but others have complimented you.

Dig into these talents by asking yourself questions. Maybe you discovered you really love taking pictures, but you rarely do it because you think you're not good at it. Don't worry about this. With practice and education, your talent will grow.

How could you use your love of photography to fulfill your purpose? Maybe you can become a wedding photographer and document this significant event in people's lives. You could also create a website that sells your photos of animals or nature. Maybe you can use your photography skills to create social media posts that grab the attention of influencers. Or you can use your talent for photography to teach others the art. Your opportunities will only be limited by your imagination and desire.

5. **What talents give you results when you do them**? What do you do that generates the results you want when you do them? If you are the one in your marketing group who easily makes great grades on each assignment, then your talent may be marketing. You can use your talent in any career or business that excites you. If you're good at innovative thinking, you love to share ideas that prompt new products. You could invent new ways of doing things or new products that change lives.

6. **What is it you do so well that you don't have to think about it**? What unique talent sets you apart? Are you great at motivating others? Use that talent as a coach, mentor, or speaker to inspire others to keep going.

Do you have a knack for technology? Use that skill to help others learn how to get the most out of their tech devices. Is your talent more a soft skill like being supportive of your friends as they go through tough times? Use that talent to become a counselor or become a minister, or a religious leader.

Whether you have hard skills or soft skills, you believe you're good at something or not, your talent helps you fulfill your purpose. Digging into what lights you up, fills you with joy, or makes you lose track of time will enlighten you about what your talents are.

Apply Your Special Talents

"I'm making explorations. I don't know where they're going to take me." – Marshall McLuhan.

Now that you've identified some of your special talents, it's time to begin finding ways to build your life around them. Not every talent needs to be the driver for a career. But your talents should be used to guide you through your life while fulfilling your purpose.

You can begin discovering using your talents for your purpose by finding what you're good at and getting creative on how to use those talents to best serve you and others. How can you tap into your special talents to make a positive impact on both humanity and the planet?

Contemplate what you've written, thought about, and discovered when you have been in self-reflection. What stands out to you as being your special talent or strength? Who you are, what you do, and how you show up in the world are all part of your special and unique talents.

Maybe you love doing something, but you think you will never be able to make a living at it. Can you turn that talent into something others can enjoy, and you can still create a great career. For example, maybe you love to paint, and you love art history, but you realize your talent is not on par with the great masters. Consider creating a business that takes groups on tours to different museums to learn about art and culture. Art is your passion, your purpose, and it matters in the lives of many people. And you get to share this passion with people every day. With this knowledge, we may choose to narrow down our college shortlists to schools in cities rich in culture with world-class museums.

Of course, not everyone can use their talents and strengths at work each day. In fact, 80% of working people all over the world are not engaged in their work. And there are multiple reasons for this. One of the key reasons is that most people are not able to use their natural talents, passions, and interests in their daily work.

If you are stifled, suffocated, or trapped in a job that keeps you from doing work you enjoy and using your talents, you aren't fulfilling your purpose on a daily basis. Learning how to incorporate your talents into your work and life puts you on a path that fulfills your purpose and leads to a life of fulfillment and happiness.

Begin exploring your talents to find your purpose. Then use those talents in a way that is unique to you to live a life that is enjoyable and fulfilling.

Exploring Your Talents - Worksheet

When it comes to discovering and achieving your life's purpose, it helps if you are extremely familiar with your special talents and strongest skills. Answer these questions to help you find your fulfilling life purpose.

What are your top 5 talents? How could each help you with your life's purpose?

1. ______________________________

   ____

2. ______________________________

   ____

3. ______________________________

   ____

4. ______________________________

   ____

5. ______________________________

   ____

What are your top 5 skills? How could each help you with your life's purpose?

1. ______________________________

   ____

2. ______________________________

   ____

3. ______________________________

____

4. ______________________________

____

5. ______________________________

____

What are your best qualities or characteristics? How will each make you memorable?

1. ______________________________

____

2. ______________________________

____

3. ______________________________

____

4. ______________________________

____

5. ______________________________

____

What other helpful qualities or characteristics do you want to develop?

1. ______________________________
2. ______________________________
3. ______________________________

4. ______________________________

5. ______________________________

Which of your talents make you feel confident and secure in your abilities? Why/How?

1. ______________________________

   ____

2. ______________________________

   ____

3. ______________________________

   ____

4. ______________________________

   ____

5. ______________________________

   ____

Which of your talents need to be developed more or enhanced?

1. ______________________________
2. ______________________________
3. ______________________________
4. ______________________________
5. ______________________________

Which of your skills make you feel confident and secure in your abilities? Why/How?

1. ____

2. ____

3. ____

4. ____

5. ____

Which of your skills need to be developed more or enhanced? Why/How?

1. ____

2. ____

3. ____

4. ____

Exploring Your Talents- Checklist

Your talents and gifts are those abilities that come to you naturally. They include the things in which you demonstrate an innate aptitude. They are also the things you do, know, or say that amaze other people. Use this checklist to help you explore your talents and skills, and abilities as you find and achieve your ultimate life purpose.

Check the items you exhibit and want to delve into more thoroughly.

- ☐ Ability to Focus
- ☐ Ability to handle Change
- ☐ Ability to make Friends
- ☐ Ability to spot new Trends
- ☐ Academics
- ☐ Accounting
- ☐ Adaptability
- ☐ Advertising
- ☐ Affiliate systems
- ☐ Analyzing the past
- ☐ Art
- ☐ Articulate
- ☐ Asking Questions
- ☐ Athleticism
- ☐ Awareness
- ☐ Bookkeeping
- ☐ Brainstorming
- ☐ Communication Skills
- ☐ Computer Literacy
- ☐ Computers / IT
- ☐ Conflict Resolution
- ☐ Creativity
- ☐ Critical Thinking
- ☐ Decision Making
- ☐ Detail Orientation
- ☐ Dexterity
- ☐ Drawing
- ☐ Empathy
- ☐ Encouraging
- ☐ Enthusiasm
- ☐ Fairness
- ☐ Financial Management

- ☐ Financial Planning
- ☐ Flexible
- ☐ Foreign Language
- ☐ Future Thinking
- ☐ Futuristic
- ☐ Graphics
- ☐ Guerrilla Marketing
- ☐ Health / Fitness
- ☐ High Energy
- ☐ Hiring / Recruiting
- ☐ Human Resources
- ☐ Identify Strengths / Weaknesses
- ☐ Imagination
- ☐ Imaginative
- ☐ Initiative
- ☐ Innovation
- ☐ Inspiring
- ☐ Insightful
- ☐ Integrity / Honesty
- ☐ Intuition
- ☐ Inventiveness
- ☐ Jokes / Humor
- ☐ Judging Character
- ☐ Judging Motives
- ☐ Juggling
- ☐ Leadership
- ☐ Learner
- ☐ Listening
- ☐ Logistics
- ☐ Magic
- ☐ Maintenance Tasks
- ☐ Making Connections
- ☐ Marketing
- ☐ Math
- ☐ Meeting Management
- ☐ Money Management
- ☐ Music
- ☐ Negotiating Skills
- ☐ Networking Online
- ☐ Networking In-person
- ☐ Organizing
- ☐ Personal Productivity
- ☐ Persuasive

- ☐ Photography
- ☐ Planning
- ☐ Positiveness
- ☐ Problem-Solving
- ☐ Programming
- ☐ Project Management
- ☐ Public Speaking
- ☐ Raise Money
- ☐ Reading
- ☐ Relaxation
- ☐ Reliability
- ☐ Relieve Stress
- ☐ Research
- ☐ Resilient
- ☐ Risk Management
- ☐ Sales
- ☐ Self-Assurance
- ☐ Self-Control
- ☐ Self-Discipline
- ☐ Self-Management
- ☐ Sign Language
- ☐ Singing
- ☐ Social Intelligence
- ☐ Social Networking
- ☐ Software
- ☐ Story Telling
- ☐ Strategic Planning
- ☐ Systems management
- ☐ Taxes
- ☐ Teaching / Training
- ☐ Time Management
- ☐ Trouble-shooter
- ☐ Typing
- ☐ Video Creation
- ☐ Visualization
- ☐ Volunteering
- ☐ Website
- ☐ Wisdom
- ☐ Woodworking
- ☐ Writing

Add your personal talents, skills, and abilities here:

- [ ] ____________________
- [ ] ____________________
- [ ] ____________________
- [ ] ____________________
- [ ] ____________________
- [ ] ____________________
- [ ] ____________________
- [ ] ____________________
- [ ] ____________________
- [ ] ____________________
- [ ] ____________________
- [ ] ____________________
- [ ] ____________________
- [ ] ____________________
- [ ] ____________________
- [ ] ____________________
- [ ] ____________________
- [ ] ____________________
- [ ] ____________________
- [ ] ____________________
- [ ] ____________________
- [ ] ____________________
- [ ] ____________________
- [ ] ____________________
- [ ] ____________________
- [ ] ____________________
- [ ] ____________________
- [ ] ____________________
- [ ] ____________________
- [ ] ____________________
- [ ] ____________________
- [ ] ____________________
- [ ] ____________________
- [ ] ____________________
- [ ] ____________________
- [ ] ____________________

Exploring Your Passions To Find Your Purpose

"If you can't figure out your purpose, figure out your passion. For your passion will lead you right into your purpose." – Bishop T.D. Jakes

If you've ever asked someone how to find your purpose, you've most likely heard the answer, "Follow your passion." Every person has passions: We're passionate about our hobbies, our beliefs, our family, and our work. Many find passion in helping others, caring for the environment, creating content, or taking care of animals.

How can these passions help you find your deeper purpose? By exploring your passions, those things that give you a sense of joy, happiness, and fulfillment, are all insights into discovering your purpose in life. Passion and purpose can be aligned, but not all of your passions will lead to your purpose.

Following your heart or passion has its benefits and can change your life by including the following:

- More joy and happiness.
- A feeling of excitement in your life.
- More fulfillment in all areas of life.
- Stronger and healthier relationships.
- Less fear, worry, anxiety, and stress.
- Being more comfortable with life's ups and downs.
- More opportunities will come your way.

Passion and purpose are key components of the fulfillment equation. Passion is about emotions, motivation, and what makes us feel good. It's the "love what you do" part of the equation. Purpose, on the other hand, is "the why" driving force behind what we do.

Passion can range from silly to exciting. Purpose is focused and intentional. Passions come and go while your purpose tends to be around a lot longer, evolving as you grow and mature. Passions are inward reflections, while your purpose is outward, focusing on the greater impact you have on others or on your community.

Passion can be a direct part of your purpose. In fact, when your passion and purpose are closely aligned, you are more likely to be fulfilled.

In fact, aligning your purpose, passions, and your talents is the key to long-term fulfillment.

Let's say that you have identified your purpose and you want to inspire people and make positive changes in their lives. You are also passionate about living a minimalistic lifestyle. You have also discovered that writing is your big talent. One way you can create a life that is fulfilling for you would be by blogging, writing books, creating training programs, etc., around your passions. All of these ideas are a way you could create an impact of change on the global community while making a great financial living at the same time.

Passions are normally easy to identify and can sometimes be identified based on your purpose. But for most people, exploring your passions will lead to finding a deeper purpose. Sometimes the things we do just bring us fun and pleasure, but they are not fulfilling our true purpose. If this is the case, the idea is to begin digging deeper into your talents, your values, and the areas where you can impact the world.

In this book, I will guide you step by step through the process of evaluating, reflecting, and discovering your passions. In the end, all this work will help you understand your purpose.

Harness Your Passion

"Always remember, you have within you the strength, the patience, and the passion to reach for the stars to change the world." – Harriet Tubman.

Do you know anyone who has a very unusual passion? Maybe it's spiders, turtles, or digging caves like sculptor Ra Paulette, who digs caves and shapes them into works of art. Maybe you are aware of a unicycle-riding actress like Leslie Mann. Each of these passions may appear to be hobbies. But what if their activities were connected to their underlining purpose?

Digging caves for Paulette is about changing the way people see art. Unicycling isn't Leslie Mann's purpose; it's a hobby driven by passion. Your passion can lead you to change your life. It can provide the motivation to change the lives of others. It can fill your life with excitement and inspires those around you.

I love to visit arts and crafts festivals while I travel. As I write this, my wife Karen and I are vacationing in Fripp Island, South Carolina. Yesterday we spent some time in downtown Beaufort, walking the waterfront and enjoying "The Taste of Beaufort Festival." Two particular vendors stood out to us. The first was a couple that lived part of the year on their sailboat in the Caribbean Islands. They search the beaches and waters for sea glass which they then turn into one-of-a-kind jewelry. They spend the rest of their year living the "van life," traveling to shows around the country, selling their jewelry at different festivals, and using social media to sell jewelry on their own website. Their niece manages the fulfillment for them while they travel the world. I don't know how much money they make, but they are amazingly happy and fulfilled with their lives.

The next vendor that stood out to us was an artist who printed maps on wood. These maps reflect the local areas where they were displaying their work. The artist would add a unique touch to the art by adding characters like a crab, dolphin, or turtle. Her mom and dad both worked with her, and after four years, she does about 20 shows a year, and her work is in over 500 retail locations around the country.

She had found a way to express her artistic talents to the world and created a thriving business at the same time.

To harness your passion for a larger purpose, you first need to know what that passion is. Let's look at how you can start to do that.

Listening to yourself. The vast majority of people simply go through the motions of their day. All the constant demands on them cause them to make the easiest choices without thinking too much about most of them. This is what I call following the path of least resistance. To leverage your passion, you will need to discover what you want. You just need to slow down a bit so you can spot the clues about what excites you and not quickly dismiss them as a childhood fantasy.

Listen to what makes you daydream. Asking yourself these questions can help you discover your life passion.

1. If you never had to work, how would you spend your time?
2. What are your natural talents and skills?
3. What would you not want to ever give up or stop doing?
4. What do others ask you about?
5. Why do you enjoy the hobbies you have?
6. Are there things you do better than most?
7. What makes you curious?
8. What do you spend your money on?

Take your time. It takes time to discover your passions. If you want to grow and have something more than what you currently have, you will need to get uncomfortable and step into areas that aren't familiar to you. You will have to be willing to pay the price to be able to pursue your purpose. That means sacrificing some things while you follow your dream. Prepare for setbacks, roadblocks, and disappointments along the way. But remind yourself of why you want this and know the sacrifice will be worth it. You will need to become the best version of yourself. The skills you have now will need to be developed and grown to be the best version of yourself.

Discovering and developing your passions will lead you toward living your purpose and having a fulfilling life. Passionate people are visionaries, persistent, and happy. Following your passions will allow you to discover ways to light up the world.

Explore Your Passions

"There is no passion to be found in playing small—in settling for a life that is less than the one that you are capable of living." – Nelson Mandela.

There are many ways to explore what your passions are and how they relate to your purpose. Many may seem silly or time wasters, but once you begin the journey of exploring your passions and doing the work, you'll see the results.

Meditation Opens the Subconscious

Mention the word meditation, and the images of some new-age yogi quickly come to mind for many, but nothing could be further from the truth. Meditation and brain research have been rolling in steadily for some years now, and it seems like a new study is coming out almost every week that highlight some new benefits of meditation.

Did you know many famous and successful people credit meditations for their ability to gain focus, reduce stress, and energize themselves? Arnold Schwarzenegger, Steve Jobs, Oprah Winfrey, Jerry Seinfeld, Lady Gaga, Russell Simmons, Ellen DeGeneres, Cameron Diaz, Clint Eastwood, Katy Perry, and many more all practice meditation.

For those of you not impressed by the habits of the rich and famous but driven by hard facts and science, this is for you. Forbes magazine reported that a group at Harvard discovered that mindfulness meditation actually changes the structure of your brain. It turns out that eight weeks of Mindfulness-Based Stress Reduction (MBSR) increase the cortical thickness in the hippocampus. The hippocampus regulates memory and learning, and in some areas of the brain, that plays a part in emotion management and self-referential processing. The research also showed a reduction in brain cell volume in the amygdala. The amygdala, you may recall, is responsible for anxiety, stress, and fear. The results were aligned with the participants' self-reported levels of stress. Meditation not only changes the structure and responses of your brain, but it also changes your own perception and feelings as well.

In fact, a follow-up study found that after meditation, changes in brain areas linked to mood and arousal also resulted in improvements in how participants reported they felt — i.e., their psychological well-being.

So, what is meditation? Although there are many types of meditation, at its core, meditation is about reaching a level of peace and silence effortlessly. With meditation, you will feel centered, calm, and refreshed. And while there are lots of forms of meditation, one of the most prevalent forms of meditation is Transcendental Meditation, or simply TM.

Initially, when you're first starting out, you will need a quiet environment. As you gain more experience in meditating, you will be able to do it anywhere despite any noise and distractions. However, when you first begin, silence is extremely helpful.

Assume a comfortable sitting posture. You could sit on a chair, bed, or floor. The key point to note is that transcendental posture is a seated position. You do not do transcendental meditation while lying down. The goal is to meditate and not drift off to slumberland.

With just about all the different types of meditation, there is a need to focus. The need to focus usually stresses people out further because they often find their minds racing with a million different thoughts in their heads while they're trying to meditate. This mental racing is very normal. Even experienced practitioners face this challenge. It takes practice to silence your mind and not anchor on your thoughts. With the TM technique, there is no need to concentrate or focus. Transcendental meditation is designed to be natural and effortless.

Once you're in a seated position, you can place your hands on your lap or by your side. Next, you will chant a rudimentary sound that doesn't have any meaning. You do not want the sound you make to conjure any thoughts or images. The sound you make could be an "aaaaahhh" or "ummmmmm." It doesn't matter what the sound is as long as it's comfortable for you. The simple sound you make is called a mantra or chant. Imagine all your thoughts revolving around your chant. The chant is like a cone swirling downwards. Initially, you may have thoughts continually popping up. Do not try to stop or force your thoughts to fade away. The key is not to make an effort here but to let the process unfold naturally. Keep focused on your chant as it leads you down the path where there is little thought.

When your mind drifts, gently guide it back by focusing on your mantra. As a little time passes, your thoughts will gradually slow down and even diminish. You can't force this process. It will happen naturally with time.

When you enter the "zone," the place where there is little thought, you will observe the tension in your body starts to dissipate. You will begin to notice your heart rate slowing, and you might even experience a light tingling sensation in your hands and feet. All this is very normal. Once you enter the zone, you want to try and stay in the zone for around 20 minutes. Any thoughts that form here will typically dissolve away. When returning thoughts start running amiss, refocus on your mantra and return to the zone.

That pretty much sums it up. Aim to do this twice daily – Once in the morning and once later in the day or early evening. Here are a few quick tips.

1. Wear loose, comfy clothing and sit in a comforting location.
2. Shut your eyes and focus on a relaxing thought, phrase, or image.
3. You will find that thoughts pop into your head. This is quite normal. Just try not to dwell or anchor your focus on these thoughts. Return your focus to your image or sound.
4. If you find you are still having trouble, try playing relaxing music during your meditation.

5. As you continue with your practice, it will begin to feel natural, and you will become more relaxed.

Meditation is a learned skill that does require you to take the time and effort to master it. But once you do, you can use it to become relaxed and focused, and this will help you on your path to discovering your life purpose. If chanting a sound seems a bit distracting or awkward to you, you can alternatively focus on your breathing. Here's a quick overview of an alternative meditation approach:

1. Sit in a peaceful place with no distractions. The best sitting position is one where you are comfortable without having to change positions. This can be a firm, comfortable chair or on a mat in the lotus position if you are able to.
2. Focus on your breathing. Feel how the air is moving in through your nose and the feel of the exhale out of your mouth. Remain focused on your breathing for at least 10 minutes. When you find your mind starts to wander, bring it back to focusing on your breathing. It will take practice.
3. As you sit quietly, ask yourself, "Why am I here? What is my purpose in life?" Then just return to focusing on your breathing, relaxing, and listening to the answers.
4. Meditate every day to repeat the process. It can take several days to find the answers to your questions. Create a mediation schedule and continue asking the appropriate questions until you receive an answer that makes sense intuitively to you. The correct answer will simply feel right to you.
5. Use guided meditation if you need help with your meditations. There are many videos on YouTube that have meditations. Many find guided meditation easier, especially for someone just starting to meditate. There are other products and apps you can use as well, such as books and audio programs on meditation. Experiment until you find an approach that works for you.

Journaling as a Way to Discover your Deep Purpose

"How we spend our days is, of course, how we spend our lives." – Annie Dillard.

Maintaining a journal is one of the best ways to get to know yourself on the deepest level. It reveals your inner thoughts, feelings, and desires. Journaling allows you to connect with who you are, helping you discover things about yourself you never knew before. By learning about yourself, you discover what you really want in life and what your passion is.

Many people find starting a journal daunting. It's difficult to know how to use journaling as a self-discovery tool, let alone know where to start. Begin with these ideas to help you get started in the self-discovery journaling process.

- **Write down your doubts, fears, anxieties, and worries**. Fears and doubts, worries and anxieties manifest into much bigger problems in your mind if you don't deal with them. Bottling up your emotions and thoughts makes them begin to feel a lot worse than they really are. Writing them down in a journal gets them out of your head. It gives you a chance to discover new ways to resolve them.

  As you journal about them, you can look closer at the fears and doubts. Explore where they are coming from without judgment. You may shock yourself with how much more you learn about yourself and your ability to overcome your fears, worries, doubts, and anxieties in your life.

  For each fear you have written down, I want you to ask these three questions:

  1. What is the worst thing that could potentially happen?
  2. What would you do if the worst thing occurred?
  3. Are you ok with the worst thing occurring?

  If the answer to question three is yes, they commit and move forward and don't think about that fear again.

Let's look at an example I had recently with a graduating student. The student wanted to start a non-profit but was scared he would not be able to raise enough money to draw a small paycheck.

I asked what the worst thing that could happen if he actually could not raise the money? He would lose a year working and the income and experience he would have gained.

I asked what he would do if he was not successful in raising funds? He said he would go get a job.

I asked if he was ok losing a year of income and experience in a job to pursue his dream. He said without hesitation… YES.

By asking yourself what the worst thing that could happen and working through the scenarios, you are moving your fear from an abstract concept to a specific risk. You can then deal with those specifics in a logical manner that frees you from the stress of uncertainty.

- **Journal about your passions, the things that make you happy and bring you joy.** Concentrate your thoughts on the positive things in your life as well as your journey of self-discovery. Focusing solely on the negative aspects of your life won't be helpful in the long term. Instead, write about the things you enjoy.

  Write down what you were passionate about as a child, what you enjoy doing now, have always enjoyed but no longer do, or would love to learn to do. Identify what you are passionate about. This helps you discover what makes you happy. Once you know that, you can make a plan and follow it to do more of whatever that is.

  Don't forget to journal about the things you're grateful for as well. This works especially well if you're having trouble thinking positively since it automatically improves your mindset.

- **Journal in the third person format**. This might feel a bit strange to do but writing in the third person actually helps you see solutions by distancing you from the issue. This allows you to be able to look at the issue from a different perspective.

  Start writing in the third person for any issues you can't resolve. What advice would you give someone in the same situation? Use the third-person narrative to explore your passions that lead to a deeper purpose in life. It's a kind of "act as if" type of writing that lets you become someone else, often releasing the passions that are true for you.

- **Use prompts in your journaling to become self-aware**. There are several you can use. For example, look at your favorite inspirational quotes. Now create an entire journal page about it.

Ask yourself questions to prompt your writing. "What do I feel is missing from my life?" "If money was no object, what would you do with your life?" If you knew there was no way you could fail, what would you do?" "Who is the most interesting person you would want to have lunch with? List five reasons you find them interesting. "What is something you would want to be remembered for?" "Where would you love to live and work?" "What is your biggest fear in life?"

These are a few to get you started, but any deep questions that require well-thought-out answers are the questions that will help you discover more about yourself.

Open Up To Creativity

"The crowning fortune of a man is to be born to some pursuit which finds him employment and happiness, whether it be to make baskets, or broadswords, or canals, or statues, or songs. – Ralph Waldo Emerson

As a child, you most likely played make-believe or made-up rules for games you played. You might have dreamed up your own characters or talked to your stuffed animals as if they were alive.

As young adults, we start to obsess over what other people will think of us or of our ideas. We start to lose our ability to be creative. Creativity is necessary as a part of exploring your passion when you want to find a deeper purpose. It's not only part of creating art or building something but necessary for deciphering how to use your passion as a part of your purpose.

You can tap into your creativity in many ways. Bring it to the surface when you need it and use it often. Here are eight ways to tap into your creativity.

1. **Take a walk and meander aimlessly**. Put away your phone. Be aware of where you are and where you are headed. Then just walk, not worrying about anything else. Notice the things around you, the people, the scents, the colors. Let your mind just wander and take note of the thoughts you are having.

2. **Dance by yourself in the dark**. Relax and enjoy the feeling of how you move. Let your body and mind connect. Dancing is a creative outlet for your body. Doing so in the dark lets you freely dance and not think or worry. This opens up your creative blocks to see where your passions lie.

3. **Create a list of ten or more really awful ideas**. Letting yourself fail and look bad helps you tap into your creativity and to see where you don't want to be. Follow up with a list of ten original ideas or creative ideas on how to follow your passions.

4. **Connect with your inner child**. What did you do for fun? Did you jump rope? Race on your bike? See figures in the clouds or build rocket ships in the sand? Be still and listen to your inner child. Let your inner child lose by swinging on a swing, playing checkers, or lying in the grass, looking at the clouds.

5. **Open up to your creative side by creating a unique solution to a problem.** List the problems in one column and the creative ways to attack each one. This allows your mind to open up to creative thinking.

6. **Color like a kid**. Coloring is a great way to boost your creative side, and it has the added benefit of relaxing you. There are many great adult coloring books out there, so grab one and a pack of colored pencils. Find a quiet place and just color. Coloring calms you and gets you into a meditative state, perfect for allowing your creative thoughts to come to the front of your mind.

7. **Try a new skill that will spark your creativity**. This allows you to be open to learning and trying something different. When you are open to learning, you are being creative in finding a passion that could be a part of your purpose. Take a guitar lesson or sign up to learn how to build a birdhouse. Pick up snowboarding or tennis. Learn how to fly fish or take a cooking or art class.

8. **Indulge in listening to a podcast you wouldn't normally listen to**. Listen to a political show, followed by a motivational show, followed by a business or cooking show. This opens up your mind and inspires you to follow your own passions.

Tapping into your creativity opens you up to learning what lights you up. When you change the way you do something or spend time alone with your own thoughts, you are able to tap into your creative side. Once you are open to your creativity, you can imagine the ways your passion will give you a deeper purpose in life.

Ask Yourself

If you are struggling to figure out how your passions are part of your deeper purpose? Ask yourself these questions and take action on them:

1. Look deeply at what you're drawn to in life. What do you read? What do you watch or listen to? Who do you follow?
2. What upsets you or annoys you in the world? What compels you to do something?
3. Who are the people that inspire and uplift you? Where are they? What are they focusing on?
4. What college-level course or program would you take if it were free?
5. In what ways are you drawn to helping others?

6. What problems or mistakes in your life can be turned into a message for others?
7. What skill or talent do you think would be exciting to learn that you don't have?
8. What do you secretly fantasize about being involved in but feel foolish acting on?
9. If you knew you couldn't fail, what would you try?
10. What are the things you enjoyed doing when you were younger, but no longer do?
11. What beliefs hold you back that keep you from pursuing what excites you to your core?

Which of these can you take action on now to begin following your passions for your purpose? What actions will you need to take to make them happen?

Explore What Makes You Curious

"I don't know what I am. I know that I am not a category. I am not a thing - a noun. I seem to be a verb, an evolutionary process." – R. Buckminster Fuller.

Most of the time, people start to become stressed when they are thinking about finding their passion and following their purpose. When they feel lost and are focused on the answer and not the process, they feel pain, frustration, and anguish. Stop for a moment, and let's explore what makes you curious and happy. You can achieve this by asking yourself questions, trying new things, meditating, and journaling.

What kinds of posts, stories, videos, or people grab your attention? What topic or causes moves you? What content keeps you continually engaged to the very end? This is where your curiosity lies. When something gives you a feeling of wanting to know or learn more, of wanting to lean in a little more, dive a bit deeper, this is when you have discovered your interests and potential foundation for your passions.

What would you like to spend more time on? Instead of focusing on what you are missing or don't have, focus on what you do have.

Maybe your purpose is something you already do. But you aren't doing it because you don't have the time or resources or you think there is no way to make any money off it. If it's a passion, figure out how you can implement it more into your day-to-day life. How can you make the time or find the resources to allow you to do that passion you already have?

What topic would you talk about if you only had 20 minutes to talk about a topic with no preparation? Think deeply about this one. This is the question that reveals what comes naturally to you.

____

____

What energizes you? What lights your fire?

____

____

What can you talk about for hours, losing track of time?

____

____

What do you talk to your friends about that you don't believe is a passion or your purpose?

____

____

Answer these questions, and you'll be on the right track to finding your life purpose. Let's dive a little deeper by completing the Exploring Your Passion Worksheet.

Exploring Your Passion- Worksheet

Discovering your purpose can be a difficult and time-consuming journey. However, if you know what you are most passionate about, your passion can help to point you toward your life purpose. Answer the questions and provide the related information in the worksheet to help you narrow down the field.

In society, what 6 things (prioritized) make you angrier than anything else in the whole world? Describe in detail why each thing makes you so angry.

1. ____

   ____

   Why?

   ____

   ____

   ____

2. ____

   ____

   Why?

   ____

   ____

   ____

3. ____

   ____

   ____

Why?

4.

Why?

5.

Why?

6.

Why?

What 6 things (prioritized) make you happier and feel more fulfilled than anything else? Describe in detail why each thing makes you feel so fulfilled and joyful.

7. ____

____

Why?

____

____

____

8. ____

____

Why?

____

____

____

9. ____

____

Why?

____

____

____

10.

Why?

11.

Why?

12.

Why?

List all of the things and "causes" that you are passionate about.

1. ______________________
2. ______________________
3. ______________________
4. ______________________
5. ______________________
6. ______________________
7. ______________________
8. ______________________
9. ______________________
10. ______________________
11. ______________________
12. ______________________
13. ______________________
14. ______________________
15. ______________________
16. ______________________
17. ______________________
18. ______________________
19. ______________________
20. ______________________
21. ______________________
22. ______________________
23. ______________________
24. ______________________
25. ______________________
26. ______________________
27. ______________________
28. ______________________
29. ______________________
30. ______________________
31. ______________________
32. ______________________
33. ______________________
34. ______________________
35. ______________________
36. ______________________

My Personal Notes

Exploring Your Passion – Checklist

Passion can look and feel differently in each person. Just because you aren't always jumping for joy about everything you like doesn't mean you aren't passionate. In this case, this checklist will help you explore and identify a variety of things that may trigger strong emotions within you. Check off the items when you have explored them fully.

What things do you love doing and do them enthusiastically?

____

____

____

What do you enjoy doing so much that you are driven to put off other things for it?

____

____

____

What excites you so much that you can't wait to get started on the task/project?

____

____

____

What circumstance or event disturbs you so much that you want to help others fix it?

____

____

____

What things sadden you and touch your heart so deeply that you tend to cry?

____

____

____

What would most of your friends identify as your favorite things to do?

____

____

____

What makes you feel good about yourself and confident in your knowledge or skill?

____

____

____

If you never had to work, what would you spend most of your day doing?

____

____

____

What holds your interest longer than anything else?

____

____

____

You are the go-to person for what information or topics?

____

____

____

What are you continually curious about?

____

____

____

Things I Love Doing

- ☐ ____________________
- ☐ ____________________
- ☐ ____________________
- ☐ ____________________
- ☐ ____________________
- ☐ ____________________
- ☐ ____________________
- ☐ ____________________
- ☐ ____________________
- ☐ ____________________
- ☐ ____________________
- ☐ ____________________
- ☐ ____________________
- ☐ ____________________
- ☐ ____________________
- ☐ ____________________
- ☐ ____________________

Ways I Can Help Others

- ☐ ____________________
- ☐ ____________________
- ☐ ____________________
- ☐ ____________________
- ☐ ____________________
- ☐ ____________________
- ☐ ____________________
- ☐ ____________________
- ☐ ____________________
- ☐ ____________________
- ☐ ____________________
- ☐ ____________________
- ☐ ____________________
- ☐ ____________________
- ☐ ____________________
- ☐ ____________________
- ☐ ____________________

Making Your Purpose A Passionate Part Of Your Life

"Follow your own passion - not your parents,' not your teachers' - yours." – Robert Ballard.

You have taken the time to explore your talents and discover your passions, and you have probably developed some really good ideas about what fills you with purpose. It is important to note that your purpose is a maturing and evolving vision as you evolve and mature throughout your life. The difference between those who are happy and enjoy life and those who seem frustrated, angry, and stressed is their ability to continue to pursue their purpose as their lives get more and more complicated. Happy people are process-focused, not outcome-focused. Happy people focus on enjoying the journey.

What's Stopping You?

The three main reasons people fail to take action are: The first reason is what I call "The Tyranny of How." The second reason is what I call "The Perfect Map," where individuals want an exact map coordinate and path forward instead of a compass. And finally, is a big one, Fear. Let's explore each one of these reasons.

There is a principle called "The Tyranny of How." This basically says that when people have a dream or a big goal, they get excited until they start to confront the process of exactly how they are going to achieve it. Since they don't yet know how they get demoralized, and procrastination kicks in. Fortunately for you, we live in a time where anyone can become an expert in almost any area, provided you are willing to do the work. Do it first, learn how second.

Most people believe they need to know exactly the who, what, why, how, and when of their purpose. This lack of 100% clarity keeps them from even starting their journey. The goal is to work your way there. I like to use the analogy of a compass vs. a GPS coordinate. The GPS coordinate will lead us to exact turn-by-turn instructions, but we might find we are moving fast on the wrong track. The compass, on the other hand, moves us forward in the direction of our purpose. It allows us to gain more experience and knowledge on our ultimate journey. These experiences and knowledge we gain will ultimately bring clarity and ensure we are moving fast in the direction of our dreams and that we are on the right track as well.

When you start on your journey, you have to realize that you are making all kinds of assumptions about the future and all kinds of things you have yet to experience first-hand. You are starting your journey at a time you know the least you will ever know about your journey. Do you really think you should be locked into a specific GPS coordinate before you get any real-world feedback? Of course not! Pick a direction and start moving, start learning, start gaining experiences, and build and refine your purpose as you evolve and mature.

Fear is perhaps the reason more people never get started on their dreams than any other reason. We fear the unknown. We fear we will fail. We fear we will let someone we love down. We fear we will disappoint. We fear that we won't have what it takes. We fear we won't make enough money. We fear we will be judged. Many even fear achieving success.

There is no step-by-step formula for overcoming your fears, but here's an approach I have found effective.

1. First, acknowledge your fear.
2. Next, Write down your fears and describe your fears as clear as possible.
3. Ask yourself what is the worst thing that can happen?
4. Decide if you can live with the worst-case scenario.
5. If you can live with the worst-case scenario occurring, move forward.
6. Commit and don't look back or second guess your decision.

One of the true keys to success is to learn to focus on the things that will drive you in the long run and ignore, eliminate, and block out the things that distract you or don't support you. When faced with a decision, ask yourself if it will move you toward or away from your purpose. Your purpose becomes a North Star guiding your decision-making and actions.

Before you can align your passions, talents, and purpose to your work, you will have to figure out how to make them a part of your life every day. Living a passionate life begins with what brings you joy, knowing what you care about and why you create the things you do.

Purpose is your why, your motive, or the justification for doing the work you do. It's purposeful work that contributes in a deeper way to the world and allows you to use your talents with passions. Following your purpose and living a life filled with passion allows you to offer value to others.

Making your purpose a passionate part of your life requires planning, focus, and discipline. It requires willpower, making a plan, and taking action. Of course, your energy can be boosted by having a healthy lifestyle that includes sleeping and eating well, getting plenty of exercise, and being present in your everyday life through meditation, prayer, or other practices.

A healthy lifestyle impacts every other area of your life. Along with a healthy lifestyle, though, is the need to take action and be aware of every choice or decision you make as it relates to your purpose.

Mind Mapping Exercise

Mind maps are a brainstorming tool that helps us gain clarity by getting ideas down on paper without the normal filtering process we tend to place on ourselves when thinking about purposeful future careers. By removing our judgment, we can identify opportunities that we otherwise would have missed.

Mind mapping is an exercise where we use what is called a free association of words, one right after the other. This exercise is designed to open up our minds and develop creative solutions. The visual nature of this exercise allows our ideas and related concepts to be identified without filters. This exercise is so powerful because it allows you to generate a lot of creative ideas. And due to the visual nature of this exercise, it allows you to bypass your logical filters.

In creating our mind maps, we follow a simple four-step process:

1. Select our topic for mapping.
2. Creating the mind map itself.
3. Making secondary connections.
4. Creating concepts by mashing them all up.

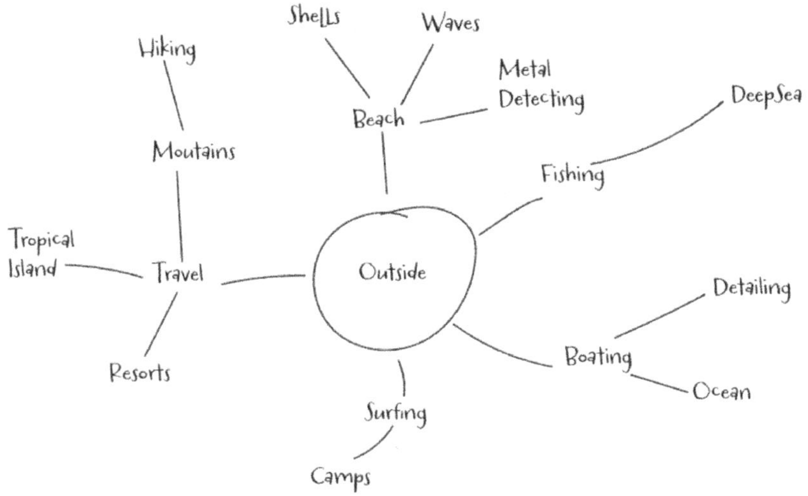

The image above is of a student's mind map, which he made while being stuck on the problem of how to find the "perfect" job. The things he enjoyed the most had something to do with being outside. He was not excited by the idea of working inside at a desk job all day. He decided to mind map ideas around being outside. He started the process by drawing a circle and writing "Outside" in the circle. This is step one.

In Step two, we are going to start our mind map. To do this, you will build off the center circle and write down five or six things that are related to your central idea. Don't think about this too much. Just write down the first five or six related ideas that come to mind.

In my student's example, he wrote down the beach, fishing, boating, surfing, and travel. All of these ideas are connected to his central idea of being outdoors. Using these words, create new branches for a new set of word associations.

When creating your mind map, give yourself a time limit, say no more than five minutes. The idea here is you don't want to think about it too much and start applying your personal limiting filters to your ideas.

The next step in our process is to highlight a few of the words that seem to really stand out to you. The further away from the center of your mind map, you will typically find some of your best ideas. As you move further from the center of your mind map, typically, the less concise thinking you have applied and your most creative ideas have emerged.

The next step is to take these words and start developing possible career or business ideas. Could he work during the summer on a charter fishing boat, at a surf camp, or at a local resort on the beach? Could he work at a camp for kids focused on the outdoors? Could he work as a fishing guide for a destination travel company? My student is no longer lost. In fact, he now has created more ideas to research than he ever imagined.

Focus on Small Changes

> *"If you feel like there's something out there that you're supposed to be doing, if you have a passion for it, then stop wishing and just do it."* – Wanda Sykes.

Now that you're eager to live a life of purpose, you're passionate and filled with the energy to take the next big step. Take a deep breath before you jump to keep from getting overwhelmed.

The key is to focus on making little incremental changes in your habits. Making slow progress is the most reliable way to create any type of change in your life. Just like when you are trying to reach a new goal, running a marathon, for instance, you set small milestones on the path to the big goal.

Start with the end first and look to the future. What does the end of your journey look like? How do you see your ideal future? What does your life look like? With the end game in mind, we can start to build a plan to get there.

What things could you do today to get started on your purpose? Do you need to make a new plan or set some new goals? Are there people who you need to connect with? Is there anything you can do now to move you in the direction of your passion? What resources will you need to ensure you can achieve your goals?

Each morning and evening, remind yourself of your purpose, look to the future, and feel the excitement. You can do this by rereading your goals, creating a vision board of your life purpose goal, or simply journaling about it each day. Make sure to track your progress. Keep a journal to track your wins and losses. Reflect on how you can create more success and prevent future failures? Once students figure out their purpose, they can often become very impatient. They can't wait to get out of school and start living their dreams. Stay patient and learn to appreciate the journey along the way.

Communicate to others your purpose. Tell others what you want to achieve. Practice incorporating daily activities that move you closer to your passions. How can you communicate the importance of your purpose to others? You are the messenger, not just a worker pursuing your purpose. When you share your goals, people know exactly how they can help you. You will be surprised how many people will want to help you once they understand where you want to go.

For example, if you know your life purpose is to create happiness in other people's lives through your music, your plan might include teaching others to play an instrument, taking others to festivals, or hosting a tour of the local music scene. During the process, you will meet people who were once where you are now; they will naturally want to mentor you and give back. Successful people love sharing their lessons learned with others.

Put in the work. Don't expect your life purpose to magically happen. In order to turn your life purpose into a reality, it is essential to take proactive steps and implement necessary actions. Making a meaningful impact and embracing your purpose requires dedication and patience. Instead of feeling overwhelmed by the grandeur of your dreams, break them down into manageable tasks. Dedicate some time each day to work towards them, and you'll be pleasantly surprised by how quickly you start seeing results.

One of the things you want to do is interview people who are in a position where you would like to be. Ask for their insights and advice. Ask them where the big challenges are. Asking them what advice they would give someone just starting on their journey. Success leaves clues. Learn to model success.

Visualize Your Life

Visualizing your life helps by priming our brains to act to make our dreams come true. Visualizing actually living the life you want activates the same neural networks that fire when our dreams are our reality. It activates our creative unconsciousness, in other words... It's part of the process of creation.

You have likely heard of the Law of Attraction. Visualizing your life is part of this concept. What you visualize, you eventually have or create through action. Basically, it comes down to the saying,… What you believe you can achieve! Many successful people use visualization to improve themselves, reach their goals, as well as live out their purpose.

Visualizing your life is the first step in your journey to creating a life with purpose. With visualization, you can start to design your life with clarity, giving you the motivation, you need to act on your dreams.

Retired Navy Seal Commander Mark Devine, in his book "*The Way of The Seal*," describes the use of a "Mind Gym" for his visualizations. This is a room in his mind where he goes to do his mental visualizations. He envisions himself walking down a path, upstairs, and through a door to his gym. The gym is like any real room, fully furnished and decorated. The formal process of entering a room gives his mind the time to adjust and focus.

There are many ways to practice visualization: mind gyms, journaling, vision boards, writing your story, and affirmations. Let's take a look at some tips to help you get the most out of your visualization process.

1. Before you begin, write down your life meaning and purpose, as well as your passion and key goals. Think about what you desire more of in your life. Is it more money, freedom to do what you desire, love, friends, better health, more happiness, or joy? Are you looking for more adventure, to lose weight and help others along the way, or are you seeking inner peace?

2. Write a description of the passions and talents you have, want, and need to acquire to live your life filled with purpose. What qualities and values do you wish to have? Now create a clear written statement that makes your purpose a passionate part of your life.

3. Now it's time to create that vision. Use a journal or notebook to write the story of how your ideal life filled with purpose will come to be. How are you going to make it a reality? What are you doing, or how are you living right now to create that life tomorrow?

Questions to answer in your life story visualization:

- What are you doing that fills you with passion every day?
- What daily rituals and activities, habits, and routines do you do each day towards your purpose?
- How are you taking care of yourself?
- What are you doing to be better as a person and achieve your purpose?
- How are you improving relationships, building new ones, and moving into the space you need to be to live your life purpose?
- How do you spend each day living your life purpose?
- Now that you've written the story of your life purpose, you now want to create a vision board complete with pictures, images, and words that represent you achieving your dreams. Study your board daily. If you're having trouble visualizing

your life purpose, here are some tips to help you see your vision more clearly:

- Go somewhere quiet, without distractions and interruptions.
- Visit and spend time in positive places that inspire you.
- Settle yourself and get comfortable. Ground yourself in your body by taking several deep breaths and focusing on your breath. Get still and center yourself.
- Quiet your mind as if you are in meditation or prayer. Instead of focusing on your breath, as in meditation, during visualization, you focus on creating or seeing an inner mental image.

Take up to 20 minutes to do this exercise. Close your eyes and, using all your senses, create a life vision in your mind of your whole life. Notice what you see, hear, taste, smell, feel, and think,

What are you doing? Who are you with? Where are you in the country, the city, at the park, on a mountaintop? Visualize your perfect day as if it were a movie and you were the star actor. You want to experience everything in your mental image in as much vivid detail as you possibly can. Visualize your purpose. What does it feel and look like to live out your purpose?

Visualizing yourself, realizing each key goal towards your purpose. See yourself already living your ideal life. Make sure when you visualize that it's in the present, not the future. Visualize the results of your passionate efforts.

Feel the emotions you'll experience when you realize your dreams: joy, satisfaction, contentment, gratitude. Hold onto these feelings throughout your day. Practice seeing this vision repeatedly over time to make it as real as possible.

Remember that what you put out is what you get back in life. If you want a life filled with love, you must love yourself. Visualize it and live it through affirmations and intentions daily.

Avoid should. Instead, be true to yourself. It's your vision, your purpose. It doesn't include what you think you should be. Or what others think you should be or do. Visualize yourself as being your authentic self, using your gifts, talents, and passion.

When you visualize, it should not be a straight path to success and fulfillment. You need to understand you will face obstacles before they occur. You will find yourself stressed and challenged on your journey. How will you respond if you don't get into that dream school? How will you respond when you fail an exam? Struggle in a difficult class? Don't land that competitive internship? How will you respond to the host of setbacks that lay ahead? Visualize how you will deal with those inevitable setback challenges when they ultimately occur. Planning for difficulties before they occur while you are in a good headspace will lead to much better solutions and outcomes, as well as less stress and frustration.

End your visualization exercises by repeating affirmations and intentions of your vision. Repeat your visualization a couple of times a day for five or ten minutes. Your brain needs repetition to change. Be sure to do this exercise first thing each morning and right before bed in the evening. It will be difficult to do at first. Give it time, and just keep repeating it. After thirty days or so, you will be able to do it with ease. Don't give up. New habits take time, effort, and discipline to turn into long-term habits.

Translate your visualization, affirmations, and intentions into practice by taking action to make them a reality. Then begin to notice the changes in your daily life. Continue to do the visualizations and be amazed by how your life a year from now will have changed.

Living Your Purpose Everyday

Living with passion means turning off the autopilot you are running and focusing on actively creating a life that matters to you. The vast majority of students graduate high school and head off to college because that is the thing they are supposed to do. They pick a college because it is close to home or far from home, one that is affordable, or maybe they like the weather, or the football team, etc. State U has a great reputation, and all their friends are heading there, so why not go there as well.

Students are told things like every company needs managers, accountants, marketers, etc., so just pick a major that will give you lots of opportunities, so that is what many students do. College graduation finally comes around, and students go to work for that company that just happens to have a job opening and wants to hire them. Jackpot! It doesn't really matter what or where the job is because they just need to get a couple years of experience, and then they will move to their dream job anyway. Two years into that job, they get a promotion and are dating a wonderful person; they have friends in the city now, so they decide to stay put for a few more years. Before they know it, a couple of years has turned into ten or fifteen years, and they have joined 80% of the workforce disengaged and unhappy in their work. They wonder what the heck happened to them! How did they drift so far off course? They feel like there must be more to life than what they have, but they feel stuck.

The path of least resistance often looks like a blessing in the short run but rarely leads to a life of happiness and fulfillment. Life tends to happen. Before we know it, we are married, own a house, two cars, a boat, and have a couple of kids. The sensible thing to do is to stay in that secure job with that company you thought you would be with for only two years. The idea of pursuing your purpose is so far in the rear-view mirror you can't even begin to think about it. You tell yourself that you will pursue the things you are passionate about in retirement.

But it doesn't have to be that way. The way to live your purpose every day begins with getting clear on what you want, but it requires constant daily feeding and attention. Let's look at a few ways to do just that.

1. **Practicing mindfulness**. Meditation and mindfulness can help you recognize when you are lost in your own thoughts and take notice of what's going on around you. Mindfulness is the practice of staying in the present moment. It's about paying attention to the moments in your life and what's happening in the present moment in a non-judgmental way.

At the end of each day, use a journal to document your progress and discoveries, including the details of how you accomplished your purpose.

Identify your motivation each morning. What values are the most important right now? Hold this in the front of your mind like a guiding light as you move through the day. Approaching each day with what is most important to you helps you take action on the things that matter and discard what doesn't.

Practice being fully present. Foster a sense of newness to unfolding moments as if you were a child experiencing something for the first time. Take these small steps each day to help you stay aware of your purpose. When you approach your daily routines as if they were new, this perspective helps you transform ordinary actions into days filled with a greater purpose.

2. **Reframe how you see your job**. When you are engaged in what you believe is meaningful work, you take greater pride in your work, you handle stress better, and you are more likely to stay motivated.

   If your current job is less than meaningful (most college students would say yes), you might want to reframe how you see it. Ask yourself how you can think of your job in a way that makes you feel that what you're doing is meaningful.

   For example, you are a customer service quality agent for a big corporation that sells insurance to seniors. Instead of simply calling yourself a customer service agent, think of yourself as the person that helps ensure seniors are taken care of in their retirement.

3. **Choose friends who make you feel like you matter**. Friends that support you and who value you for who you are. One of the hardest things for new college students to do is leave behind childhood relationships that no longer serve them.

4. **Choose to have integrity**. Live your life following your values in ways that make you happy without causing others pain is a part of your purpose. Your values can range from being family-oriented to generosity. Core value words you might include are fulfillment, honesty, community, courage, adventure, respect, love, kindness, empathy, vitality, health, open-mindedness, and tolerance.

5. **Express yourself as you are**. Don't pretend to be someone you're not. You can't live a meaningful life if you are conforming to fit in with what others say is normal. Do your goals and actions sound like you, reflect your personality, and are in line with your values? Every action and decision should be from who you are and strive to be. They should align with your purpose.

6. **Embrace the small things**. You can help make your purpose of making the world a better place by doing small things that matter each day. Take tiny actions that can make life better for others. Depending on what your purpose is, you could rescue a dog from a pet shelter, buy the homeless snack bars, share a holiday (or any day) meal with a family that is struggling, pay it forward, share kindness, be environmentally aware, or live simply or holistically.

7. **Creating alignment through a healthy lifestyle**. Following your purpose means creating an alignment in all areas of your life. Yes, there will be sacrifices. But along the way, make sure you are including healthy choices in your process. This means eating a balanced diet, getting enough exercise, and getting plenty of sleep. And, of course, spending quality time with your family and friends while making time to care for yourself. No matter what your purpose is, it should include a healthy version of yourself. This is key to enjoying the process of reaching your goal.

Making your purpose a passionate part of your life means doing things each day from the perspective of meaning. Doing things mindfully and with a sense of purpose helps you see even the mundane everyday actions you take are a part of your purpose.

I love the story Greg Norman tells. Greg was the number one golfer in the world, but from May 1990 to September 1992, he went 27 months without winning a golf tournament. Frustrated, tired, and wondering if he should quit the game to focus on his business, he decides to go visit Jack Nicklaus. Mr. Nicklaus, at the time, was almost universally thought to be the greatest golfer of all time. Greg said that Jack said one thing that changed everything... "Purpose" What is your purpose? What is it you want to do? When you go to the driving range, what is your purpose? Just to hit balls and feel sorry for yourself because you haven't won a golf tournament in a while? Or are you going there to practice with a purpose? Greg took all this to heart, and what do you think happened? The very next week, Greg wins the tournament! In fact, Greg started playing amazingly well, and in the nine starts prior to the 1993 British Open, Greg not only won again but finished fourth or better six times. He goes on to win that British Open for his second major championship. Greg had a storied career. He was number one in the world for 331 weeks, a feat only topped later by the great Tiger Woods.

Taking The Next Steps

Making your purpose a passionate part of your life requires you to incorporate purpose into everything you do. Once you know what your purpose is and how you want it to be a part of your life, you'll find ways to lead you toward living that way.

For a purposeful life to be fulfilled, you must have consistent behavior in both your public and private life. This means acting true to your purpose and yourself, not losing focus, and finding alternative ways of dealing with obstacles. Here are a few things you can adopt to help you along the way.

- Use journaling or keeping a diary as a way to see where you are each day.
- Set goals on each step you need to take along the way.
- Focus on the small steps but remember the big picture.
- Be true to your values and authentic in your actions. Don't try to fit in. Be yourself.

- Visualize how your purposeful life looks. Use vision boards. Write your life story. Meditate for a clear picture.
- Make a plan and take the small steps needed. Find the resources you need, connect with the people who will help you, and begin taking action to get where you want to be.

Live your life with the end goal in mind. You have the image or the picture already in mind. Use it to examine every area of your life. Use it so that whatever you do on any day doesn't change your overall purpose. The end goal should be the reason you take certain steps, do things a certain way, and act the way you act. When you make purpose a passionate part of your life, it shows up in how you show up and what matters to you.

Making Purpose Part of Life - Worksheet

You've done a great deal of questioning yourself, soul searching, examining aspects of yourself, and exploring your options. Now, it's time to connect all the elements involved and infuse them into your daily life. This worksheet will help you clarify your vision and pull everything together.

Share the big-picture vision of your life purpose by describing the details of what it looks like to you and why it's so important to you and others. Include how it will affect you, the community, society, and the world at large.

My Life Purpose Vision

____

____

____

____

____

____

What life-purpose-related talents and skills do you already use in your everyday life?

___

___

___

___

___

Life-purpose-related talents and skills you need to incorporate into your everyday life.

___

___

___

___

___

Describe the talents/skills to add to your daily life and how you'll accomplish this.

___

___

___

___

___

Add Talent/Skill:

___

___

Implementation Goal:

How/Where to Implement:

Add Talent/Skill:

Implementation Goal:

How/Where to Implement:

Add Talent/Skill:

Implementation Goal:

How/Where to Implement:

Making Purpose Part of Life - Checklist

Check off each item as you complete the task and/or fill in the info or blanks. I have taken steps to complete the following tasks and meet my goals:

- ☐ Identified Life Purpose
- ☐ Listed My Passions
- ☐ Wrote Key Goals
- ☐ Identified Desires/Wants
- ☐ Listed Related Talents/Skills
- ☐ Created A Vision Board
- ☐ Go To Inspiring Places
- ☐ Quiet My Mind
- ☐ Visualize My Purpose Daily
- ☐ Set Goals
- ☐ Set Deadlines
- ☐ Listen To TED Talks
- ☐ Enhance My Skillset
- ☐ Take Action Promptly
- ☐ Journal Daily or More Often
- ☐ Practice Being Present
- ☐ Reframed Perception of Job
- ☐ Strengthen Integrity
- ☐ Develop Communication
- ☐ Maintain a Balanced Life
- ☐ Practice Life Purpose Often
- ☐ Feel & Share My Passion
- ☐ ______________________
- ☐ ______________________
- ☐ ______________________
- ☐ ______________________
- ☐ ______________________
- ☐ ______________________
- ☐ ______________________
- ☐ ______________________
- ☐ ______________________
- ☐ ______________________
- ☐ ______________________
- ☐ ______________________
- ☐ ______________________
- ☐ ______________________

I have a group of people who support and believe in me and my life purpose. I can turn to them to help me be more accountable, stay focused, provide insightful ideas/options, and much more. These people include:

Notes:

The Importance of Goal Setting

One of the strongest reasons for setting goals is that your goals provide you with a path of actionable steps toward your future. When you have goals, you have a map. You know where you want to go, and this clarity gives you motivation, energy, and a reason to get up excited and focused every day. With goals, your whole life becomes more focused and energized.

Your goal doesn't have to be something significant and impactful. Not everyone wants to pursue changing the world on a large scale. Most students want to create a life of happiness and security, and that's just fine. They want a career they like, a few good friends, and healthy life. Setting goals is about getting clear on what you want and creating a path to get there. Let's explore why goal setting is so significant in your life.

1. <u>Goals focus your life.</u>

   By getting clear on your goals, you give yourself a path to follow. With a clear sense of direction, your mind and energy are directed to a destination and prevent you from wandering aimlessly through your life. Establishing goals requires you to do some self-reflection and planning. The process of goal setting helps bring clarity and purpose to your daily actions.

2. <u>We tend to get what we measure.</u>

   Many students set a goal to simply do their best. A vague goal like this fails to give us an objective way to measure how we are actually doing. It lakes a clear benchmark for us to measure our progress at any given time. Let's say your goal is to graduate with a minimum GPA of 3.5. At any point during the semester, you can clearly measure your progress against that goal. Setting goals avoids uncertainty and helps you proceed in the right direction. Too many students set a goal of doing their best. How do you even measure doing your best? Doing your best is an avoidance mechanism to put you in a position where you can't fail. Don't be afraid to fail.

Failure is part of the success process. Failure teaches us and gives us the opportunity to grow.

3. Goals motivate you and help you keep your perspective.

When you are working toward goals, they provide you with the motivation and energy to do the difficult things you need to do on your journey. Many college students get frustrated by certain classes or assignments that just don't seem to add any value. And honestly, they are often right. But many times, they just don't see how all the dots connect. But when you focus on the end goal, you can motivate yourself through those difficult moments. You don't get caught up in the noise; you stay focused on the goal of graduation. In this regard, goals focus your energy in a positive and useful direction. Spending time complaining about why you need to take that class you don't want to take will just drain your energy and put you in a negative headspace. Better to focus on the end game and just accept there will be frustration along the way.

4. Goals provide you with a game plan.

Yogi Berra is credited with saying, "If you don't know where you are going, you might end up someplace else." Setting goals help keep our lives on the track we want to be on. Think of goals as a map or compass guiding you where you want to go. Many students struggle with this as they let their uncertainty about the future cause them to procrastinate on creating a game plan. They fall back on just doing their best. So, what do you do if you don't know exactly want you want to do? Set goals that will position you for success once you do decide. I had one student that fell in love with finance during his junior year. He wanted to go work in investment banking. The problem? He was not engaged with his education during his first two years and had a GPA of just over 2.0. If he had trusted that he would have figured out his path and done his best work, he would have been on a much better path to pursue his new dream. I see stories like this all the time. Don't put your future self behind the curve because you are not excited or motivated today.

5. Goals build your confidence.

Since our big goals require multiple smaller goals or milestones along the way to achieve our success, as we achieve and make progress along the way, we gain confidence and momentum. I learned this lesson in a strange fashion as a young golfer. I was having trouble with my putts in the five-to-seven-foot range. I went to see a professional to help with this issue, and he dropped some balls about a foot from the hole. I quickly objected and said I have no issues here. It's further out where my issues are. He explained that he wanted me to see success closer to the hole so that as we worked our way back, I would have confidence in what we were doing. Confidence is key in school, golf, and just about everything in your life. When we take even the most seemingly outlandish goal and break it into smaller manageable steps or goals, we gain the confidence we need to make our goals a reality.

6. Goals help you overcome procrastination.

Have you ever said to yourself… "I just don't feel like doing it." Whatever it was! One of the greatest success lessons you can learn in life is that it doesn't matter what you feel like doing. Success occurs from doing the things you need to do, not doing the things you want to do. Read that sentence again. Goals help reduce procrastination because goals keep you focused on what you need to do and not on what you may want to do at the moment. The secret is to break those big goals into several short-term goals or milestones that create a constant sense of urgency for you. Without these shorter milestones, your long-term goals may seem so far off that they may actually promote procrastination. As an old boss of mine was fond of saying: Take care of each day, and you take care of the week. Take care of each week, and you take care of the month. Take care of the month, you take care of the quarter, and so on.

7. Goals help you find your true north.

Most people tend to set financial or money-related goals. They believe that money will be the vehicle that allows them to do what they really want to do. In society today, there seems to be a belief that money will solve all our problems. Here is a big news flash for you. It's just not true. Money only solves money problems.

Jim Carrey, the famous actor who is worth an estimated $200 million, said, "*I think everybody should get rich and famous and do everything they ever dreamed of so they can see that it's not the answer.*"

And that is where aligning our goals with a clear understanding of our purpose plays a key role in our lives. Alignment helps us move towards the things that we truly want to achieve in our lives. Without purpose-based goals, we may find financial success but may find ourselves unfulfilled and not happy.

In order to live a life full of happiness and fulfillment, you have to figure out what is truly important to you. Throughout your life, you'll discover new and interesting things that you may never have previously been aware of. Your goals will change as you gain more experience and learn more about yourself.

Your end goal is obviously very important, but your journey is no less important. On your journey, you will discover and learn new things, have new experiences, and gain a new set of skills. Learning to embrace the process, the journey, will lead to more happiness and satisfaction in your life. Too many people wait until they achieve their final goal to allow themselves to have any fun or enjoyment. These folks often find the idea of their goal more exciting than their achieving their goal. Learn to enjoy the process, and you will have a much happier life.

I see way too many students that are in such a hurry to get their careers started that they miss out on all the nonacademic opportunities that college has to offer. Grades are important, but so are making lifelong friends, building your network, and experiencing all the social aspects college has to offer.

The Big Goal-Setting Mistake

Most people set goals backward. They focus on what they want to have. They want to be happy, make a lot of money, have a great spouse and family, etc. Here is the rub, they focus on the result, the having, not the process of becoming. They want to have a big house. They want to have an expensive car. They want to have an amazing spouse. But… They don't think to ask themselves some simple questions: What type of person do I need to become that would be attractive to that amazing future partner? What type of person do I have to become to be someone who can make a lot of money and afford all the nice luxuries the world has to offer?

The big secret to success in life is what I call the "Be, Do, Have Model. Here you laser focus on discovering who you want to ultimately Be. Next, you go about identifying and doing all the things you need to do in order to become that person. As a result of these actions, you will ultimately be able to have everything you want. When you flip the script and focus on becoming, you ultimately have what you want in life. When you focus on having, you are not living your purpose every day.

Setting Goals

Setting goals is important to the foundation of living a life of purpose. This is because goals help us fixate on our actions and put our energy toward the end goal we want to achieve. Goals bring our future into the present.

Goals are an indication of your intent to succeed. Setting goals creates an idea of where you are currently and where you want to be in the future. Setting and achieving goals affects your level of motivation, your belief, and your ability to reach your goal.

Goal setting is necessary to get you to take action and follow the steps needed to live your purpose every day. Before we dive deep into the goal-setting process, let's look at six key ingredients in the process:

1. **Set your goal**. Determine what you want to accomplish, your purpose. Then write it down. Put it onto paper. This forces your subconscious to become committed to working towards the target. Do this every morning to keep you focused.

2. **Set a deadline**. Goals need to be time-bound. You need to set a date for when you will complete the goal. Now, a life purpose goal can be anywhere from five years to a lifetime. If that seems overwhelming, break the big goal down into smaller goals that you can do more quickly.

3. **Work on your mindset**. By developing positive approaches to all aspects of your life, you can avoid getting caught up in negative thoughts and behaviors. Read inspirational books, listen to motivational people, and believe in your abilities.

4. **Develop the skills.** You will need to develop a new set of skills in order to achieve your purpose. Locate and study the best resources for gaining the knowledge, skills, and other assets you'll need to achieve your goal.

5. **Don't procrastinate**. Start by immediately taking an initial step towards your goals. It can be a simple, easy step. It just needs to be one that will get you started in the direction of achieving your goal.

6. **Keep going** until you've completed your goal. Keep the end result in mind for every action and decision you make. Stay steadfast on your goal but flexible in your tactics to achieve those goals.

Setting goals as a part of living your purpose is an important step in the process. It helps you see where you are going and what you need to do every day to get there.

Exploring SMART Goals

Setting goals is a powerful process to help bring your purpose-driven life into a reality. Without goals to guide you, you can get stuck in dreamer mode. Goals get us moving. They bring our dream future into the present. The goal-setting process helps provide you a compass directing you where you want to go in life. When you know specifically what you want to achieve, you know where you should concentrate your efforts. The SMART goal method is an extremely powerful framework to help you set effective goals. SMART is an acronym for goal setting. Here is how you can set SMART Goals for your life:

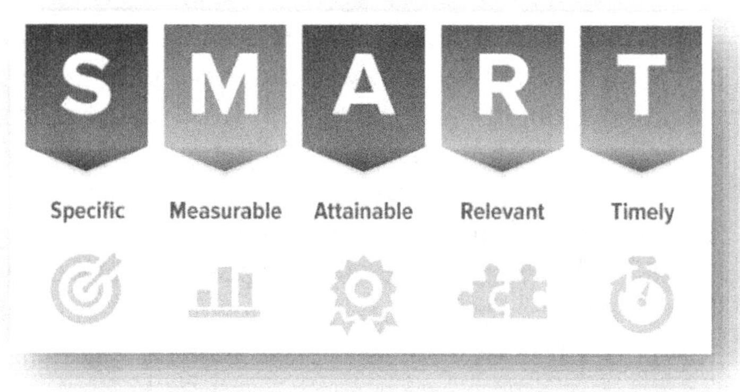

The SMART goal process creates a clear, specific, and executable framework to significantly improve your odds of achieving your goals. With this framework, each goal should be:

- **S**pecific (simple, sensible, significant).
- **M**easurable (meaningful, motivating).
- **A**ttainable (agreed, achievable).
- **R**elevant (reasonable, realistic, resourced, results-based).
- **T**ime-bound (time-based, time-limited, time/cost limited, timely, time-sensitive).

1. Specific

The first part of the framework is to ensure your goals are clear and specific. When goals are vague, you are not able to properly sequence and focus your efforts appropriately. Lack of clarity can lead to procrastination and a lack of motivation to achieve it. A quick way to test this part of the framework is to ensure your goals are:

- Clearly defined.
- Obvious to individuals who have basic knowledge in the field.

When drafting and finalizing your goals, you will want to address the five "W" questions:

- **What** do I want to accomplish?
- **Why** is this goal important?
- **Who** is involved?
- **Where** is it located?
- **Which** resources or limits are involved?

2. Measurable

Measurable goals help ensure you stay on track with your progress and will help you stay motivated. Monitoring your progress will help you maintain your focus and meet your milestones. Measuring your progress creates excitement as you move toward achieving your goals. At a high level, you want to know the following:

- If your goal is obtainable and how far away achievement is.
- When you have achieved your goal.

When you are drafting measurable goals, each goal should address questions like:

- How much?
- How many?
- How will I know when it is accomplished?

3. Achievable

For your goals to be achievable, your goals should be realistic and reasonably attainable in order for you to be successful. The idea here is that your goals should stretch your abilities but still remain achievable. Top experts say you should set your goals at the point where you have about an 80% probability of achieving the goal. This challenges you and keeps you motivated at the same time. When we set goals that are too easy, we don't need to work hard. When we set goals that are farfetched, we often give up quickly.

An achievable goal should address questions such as:

- How will I reach my desired goals?
- How practical is the goal, based on other constraints, such as financial factors, time constraints, skills, etc.?

4. Relevant & Realistic

This step in the SMART framework ensures that your goal matters to you and aligns with your other goals. Any big goals will surely require the support and assistance of others in order to achieve them. But seeking support doesn't mean we turn over the responsibility for achieving our goals. So, make sure that your goals drive everyone forward but that you're still responsible for achieving your own goal. You want to ensure your goals are relevant and realistic, taking into account the availability of resources, knowledge, and time.

Relevant goals should answer "yes" to these questions:

- Is this goal worthwhile?
- Is it the right time for this goal?

- Does this goal align with my needs?
- Am I the correct person to achieve this goal?
- Is this goal applicable given the current socio-economic environment?

5. Time-bound

Each goal that you set needs to have a target date, so you have a specific deadline for your efforts. This piece of the SMART goal framework will help ensure that your everyday tasks don't expand and take priority over your longer-term goals. You want to ensure the following:

- You have allowed enough time to achieve each goal.
- You have not allowed too much time, which would delay your achievements.

A time-bound goal should answer these questions:

- When will I achieve the goal?
- What can be done toward my goal before I go to college?
- What can I do while in college?
- What can I do after graduation?
- What can I do this year, month, or week?
- What can I do today?

Goals are the tools that move us forward in life. Goals can be thought of as the oxygen that fuels our dreams. Goals are the initial steps to every journey we take and are also our last. Given this fact, it's important that you understand the significance and importance of proper goal-setting and use this knowledge during your career and life.

A quick word of caution on setting goals. Please don't be afraid to adjust or even completely change your goals. You have to remember that the goals you set are based on your current mindset and experience. As you learn, grow, and have new experiences, you need to make sure your goals are still propelling you and not limiting you.

To get the most out of your goal setting, you should write your goals down on paper and review them each day. Focus your purpose on a single priority, the one thing you can do so that everything else becomes easier or even unnecessary. Ask yourself what the one thing is I can do today, this week, this month, or this year that can make the biggest impact toward achieving your goals.

Building Your Way Forward

You have done a lot of reflection and work at this point. Work is necessary because you can't know how to get to where you want to be until you have a good understanding of where you are. At this point, many students feel they should know exactly what they want in life. This stresses and frustrates them. Worry, fear, and anxiety are not our best discovery tools. The point here is that you don't have to have it all figured out. You just have to follow your compass for the life you want right now. This is not easy to do. We all face the gravity of following someone else compass in our lives. A big part of college goes beyond your core education and helps you answer four very important questions:

1. Who do you want to become?
2. What are things you will need to do to become who you want to be?
3. What are the things that matter most to you?
4. What is your view on work?

Ultimately, our happiest life is when our purpose, passion, and talents are in alignment. These three forces serve as our compass, guiding us toward our True North. During my early thirties, I found myself very frustrated. I was achieving all my financial goals and had a great family, but something was missing. I remember telling my wife I just felt like I was in a sailboat drifting in the middle of the ocean with no idea which land I wanted to sail toward or even where land was, for that matter. I had lost my compass! Anyone who sails will tell you can't chart a course on one straight line. When sailing, you have to take into account the currents, the tides, and the winds and chart a course based on what the conditions require. I had let my life get out of alignment. I had become so focused on a personal achievement I had completely lost track of making a positive impact on others' lives.

In building your way forward and discovering your life's purpose, I want you to think about your life as a sailboat, not a train. A train heads forward fast, controlled by where the rails allow it to go. The sailboat, conversely, must sail one way, then another, and then back the other way. Sometimes you are miles away from shore, sometimes you must hug the coastline, and still other times you must be in port. And sometimes, a big storm hits, and you find yourself completely lost, or your boat may even sink. Life is full of storms. Anytime you start to feel stuck or your life is not working, you are likely going through a significant transition. These are the times when it's important to recalibrate your compass. Double-check how aligned you are with your purpose, passion, and talents. Reassess what you value and what is important to you.

It is extremely important to realize you might not always know where you want to go, but you can always know whether you are heading in the right direction when your compass is calibrated. I find it helpful as each year comes to an end to recalibrate my compass ensuring I have not drifted too far off course.

Exercise - Why You Work

For this exercise, we are not focused on the type of work you want to do but instead on why you work. Write a short reflection (250-500 words) on your views on work. Answer the following:

Why work?

What does work mean?

What is the function of work in society?

What makes it worthwhile?

How do you view the balance between money and its impact on your work?

____

____

____

____

Finding Your Way When You Are Lost - Wayfinding

Wayfinding is an ancient practice of figuring out where you are going when you don't know your actual destination. This ancient art utilizes a compass and a heading or direction. You don't need a map or GPS coordinates. Since there is no one single destination or purpose for your life, you can't pop some GPS coordinates into your phone's GPS and get step-by-step instructions. Instead, we pay attention to the small clues, you know, the one that creates that voice in your head that says this feels off, or this seems to fit. Think about the early settlers migrating West to California in search of a better life. They just knew their current situation was not working for them, so they headed out in search of a better life. Lewis and Clark did not have a map as they set out on their journey to explore the land acquired through the Louisiana Purchase. Christopher Columbus did not have a GPS coordinate as he set out to discover new lands. They all headed in a direction, noted useful landmarks, and let the conditions create a structured path.

When undecided on a path forward, I like to ask this question: Which choice gives me the most options? Which path opens more doors or closes doors for me?

Take a student I spoke with that was struggling to decide if college was right for him. He wanted to open his own restaurant, and he just did not see how college would help with that. I asked him if his family was wealthy or if he would need investors to open the restaurant? He said he would definitely need investors. I asked him if he thought a college degree would be something he thought would add or take away from an investor's willingness to invest in him? He said he saw no way it would take away, so it would be helpful, he thought. I asked him if he thought accounting classes, marketing classes, management classes, etc., would help or hurt him in running his restaurant? Again, he acknowledges they would likely help him run a better restaurant. I asked him if he wanted to run a single restaurant or multiple restaurants. He said his dream was to build a national franchise. I asked him if going to college and being around folks who had done just that would be helpful? He said, of course, that sounds very exciting. I asked him if working in a restaurant and continuing to develop his skills while in college was possible. He said, of course. Well, you get the idea. This young man got very excited about going to college after our quick conversation.

Many times, the answer is not an either-or; it's a why not both. Many students want to start their own businesses and see college as a roadblock. After all, the Social Media guru told them how dumb it is to spend all that money on a college degree when they can become a billionaire by selling stuff online or being an influencer. I am a big fan of entrepreneurship, but unless your opportunity is extremely time sensitive think (Bill Gates and the launch of the personal computer), that business opportunity can be pursued in college while you gain the skills to scale that business venture.

Let me say here that many people are highly successful without a college degree. That is not the point I am trying to make. The point is about optionality and placing your bets where the odds increase your ability to succeed under conditions of uncertainty. I was the first in my family to go to college. My dad was a plumber, and his dad was a plumber. And by the way, I was a licensed master plumber as well. I went to college because I could play golf. I went to graduate school because I got interested in business and finance, not because I wanted to become a college professor. In fact, that career would not have made my top fifty list at the time. However, because I pursued my graduate work, it allowed me to open doors at universities that would have otherwise been closed to me. I grew up digging ditches, pumping septic tanks, and cleaning sewers, which is not your typical path to becoming a college professor and bestselling author. I am a living example of how there are many paths available to you as you search for and pursue your life's purpose. Learn to master the key decision moments in your life, and you will certainly live an uncommon life, a life full of happiness and fulfillment.

Picking A College That Fits

"There is a time when we must firmly choose the course we will follow, or the endless drift of events will make the decision for us." – Herbert Prochnow.

The Theory Of Relative Deprivation

Malcolm Gladwell is a world-renowned author of five New York Times bestsellers, speaker, journalist, and social science researcher. Gladwell has developed some controversial theories on how to pick a college that is right for you. He believes most students are better served not going to an elite college.

Gladwell believes far too many people make a college selection based on college rankings or the perceived status of an institution. When you make your selection this way, students often become what he refers to as little fish in big ponds. At these top institutions, only a few can truly stand out. Only a few will gain access to the top opportunities. He believes the vast majority of students would be better served attending universities where they could excel and be at the top of the class.

The position he takes is based on solid science. Gladwell is using the lens of "relative deception." The theory was developed by sociologist Samuel Stouffer during World War II to describe our tendency to measure ourselves against those directly around us. In essence, we compare our successes and failures to those of students in our class.

In his book *David and Goliath,* Gladwell gives the example of "Caroline Sacks" (not her real name), who was passionate about science until attending Brown University. While at Brown, her grades were average, and she felt relatively dumb compared to her brilliant straight-A classmates, despite Gladwell's estimate that she was likely in the 99th percentile globally. She eventually quit science in large part to relative deprivation.

I heard a similar story myself as a young golfer in Richmond, VA. There was a great amateur golfer at our club, and I remember asking a member why this guy had never gone pro. He told me it's the darndest thing. He said in college, there was this one kid who he could not beat. He figured if he could not beat this kid, how could he ever make a living on the PGA tour. He told me that the kid he could not beat turned out to be Jack Nicklaus, the greatest golfer of his era and some would say ever. If that is not relative deception at work, I am not sure what is.

Gladwell cites other examples and says that the worst STEM students at Harvard are likely as smart as the top third at lower-ranked colleges. He says it is eventually that the top Harvard students will make the bottom third feel like they are dumb and cannot be successful. They will have their dreams and self-confidence bruised and crushed by swimming in the big pond. It is much better, he says, to go swim in a smaller pond where they could have excelled.

Based on his work in "*David and Goliath*," Gladwell's advice would almost surely be to go somewhere where you can excel. "Rarely do we stop and consider," he writes, "whether the most prestigious of institutions is always in our best interest." In academia particularly, he says, "The Big Pond takes really bright students and demoralizes them."

Gladwell's work is certainly worth noting, as his assertions and conclusions are well-researched and supported. However, they are a bit one-dimensional and oversimplified. Let's take the case of Caroline Sacks. We have no way of knowing if she would have stayed with science at another less prestigious school. We have no way of knowing if her Ivy League degree outside of science served her better than a degree in science from a lesser-known school. We have no way of knowing what doors would not be open to her in her life if she had chosen another path.

It is important to discuss Gladwell's work as it is so widely cited and referenced. But it should not be taken as gospel. And being the big fish in a small pond might not serve you best. For instance, the advantages of an Ivy League school education go beyond the quality of your learning. They include the prestige the degree brings to you, the world-class facilities you have access to, the association with like-minded students, and perhaps most importantly, the amazing alumni network.

It is just as important that we don't choose a small or lesser-known school so we can be big fish in a small pond. Let's face it, many top companies only have intern programs with top schools. Many hiring managers take the perspective that they will hire graduates from top schools. After all, the schools already did the hard screening work for them.

Now that we covered one of the big debates in selecting a college that makes sense for you. Let's go ahead and look at the most important factors you need to consider when you choose a college.

Factors to Consider When Choosing a College

There are lots of really good colleges out there, so it can certainly feel overwhelming when you start the selection process. Given so many great choices, it really is important to hone in on the factors that will drive your decision. One of the mistakes that students and parents make in their initial screening process is to eliminate expensive schools early in the selection process.

When viewing a family's ability to pay for college, there is actually a dollar amount that colleges and governments use, and it's called the Expected Family Contribution (EFC). The EFC can level the playing field for you between what the published tuition rate is and what you will actually pay.

The EFC is based on a federal government formula and is used to allocate the money available for financial aid in any particular year. It is far from a perfect assessment, and it's not the final word on what you will pay, but it is a widely used number. This need analysis system assumes that the family has the primary responsibility for paying for college and provides help only where family finances fall short. Often more expensive schools will have more levers to pull when offering students financial aid packages. In other cases, highly competitive schools may be very stingy in their financial aid packages. It is best to just let the process play out so you can make apple-to-apple comparisons.

Regardless of your college selection, you must learn a few basic terms that will be used over and over during the process, as well as typical timelines you should be aware of. Each university is a little different, so make sure to be aware of their timelines and deadlines. Here are the big ones:

Cost of Attendance (COA): Also known as the student budget, it includes not just tuition but fees, room, and board, supplies, allowances for books, transportation, and personal and incidental expenses.

Expected Family Contribution (EFC): The annual dollar amount that your family is expected to pay toward a student's educational costs. EFC is based on family income, the net value of assets, the number of children in college, and family size.

Financial aid package (FAP): The financial aid package is a combination of various forms of student aid (grants, scholarships, loans, and employment) offered by a college and other sources to meet a student's financial needs.

Free Application for Federal Student Aid (FAFSA): A single, free application form designed by the federal government that most students must complete to apply for most forms of financial aid. It is the basis of awards by the federal and state governments and colleges as well. It is available online at www.fafsa.ed.gov.

Merit-based aid: Financial aid based on academic, athletic, artistic, or other merit-oriented criteria.

Need-based aid: Financial aid is based on the student/family's financial need, the difference between the cost of attendance, and your expected family contribution. This is the gap between total college costs and your ability to pay.

Need analysis: The process used by the government and colleges to determine a student's financial need.

Student Aid Report (SAR): A report that summarizes the information included in the FAFSA, states your EFC, and must be provided to your school's office of financial aid.

Managing Your College Selection Timeline

Two Years Before College

While some students will start the college planning process earlier, it is important to start exploring schools that interest you a couple of years before your attendance date. At this point in the process, don't filter based on cost or acceptance rates, or any other factors. We just want to start identifying schools that seem interesting to you. We will have plenty of time to filter our list later, so dream a little here.

During this discovery process, talk to your parents, guidance counselor, coaches, mentors, etc., about options they think would be a good fit for you.

During your junior year, you should take the PSAT. The PSAT is a great feedback tool for you to use in preparation for the SAT or ACT. The PSAT traditionally serves as a qualifying test for the National Merit Scholarship competition.

Your junior year is an excellent time to start asking for letters of recommendation from your teachers, coaches, counselors, employers, etc. When asking for the recommendation, provide them with bullet points they can use to jog their memory about your performance inside and outside the classroom. The easier you can make it for someone to write your recommendation letter, the more likely it will get done and cover the things you want it to cover.

One of the common mistakes students make is waiting until the end of their senior year to start looking for scholarships. Please start the process early. A recent study of incoming college students showed that over half of the incoming class had waited too long to apply for scholarships. Many scholarships require a bit of work to apply for, and deadlines are all over the map. By planning ahead, you can optimize your application process and financial aid awards.

Below is a high-level overview of the college planning process. Make sure to work with your high school counselor and college admission offices to make sure you are aware of all the specific requirements. Things often change from year to year and college to college.

The Year Prior to College

Summer Before Your Senior Year

The summer before you begin your senior year is a great time to go visit a few colleges and get a feel for the campus and surrounding community. While statistics, reputation, and programs may drive your visits, nothing replaces actually walking the grounds and visiting the different buildings and amenities, and talking with faculty, staff, and students. Most colleges schedule campus tours through their admissions office. Visit your prospective college admission website for all the information you will need to coordinate your trip.

September

By September of your senior year, you will want to start the college application process. If you haven't visited colleges yet, you will want to start that process now.

Before filling out your FASFA in January, you will want to Calculate your Expected Family Contribution (EFC) by visiting https://studentaid.gov/aid-estimator/. This calculator will let you know how much money your family could be expected to pay for college if your selected college is able to provide financial aid to help meet the fully determined financial need.

It's always a good idea to start your search for scholarship money early. Scholarships all have different timelines and qualifications, so the sooner you start looking, the more prepared you will be. Here are a few of the top websites featured by Forbes that will help you locate scholarships you may be eligible for:

1. Scholarships.com - Scholarships.com has numerous search categories for you to select from. These categories include things like your GPA, ethnicity, artistic ability, military status, SAT and ACT scores, and state of residence. The Scholarship.com subcategories will help you find niche awards that are likely less competitive.

2. Fast web - The Fastweb.com site aggregates scholarships from lots of different scholarship directories. You will be asked to create a user profile to search for scholarships. Fastweb will send you alerts when a new scholarship matching your screening is posted. The site will also notify you of any upcoming deadlines.

3. College Board - Create your account at CollegeBoard.org, you can search for awards by interests, field of study, club affiliations, or specific life situations. Based on the profile you create; the site will also match you with scholarships you are likely eligible for.

4. Going Merry - Many scholarships require the same basic information, so GoingMerry.com lets you type in your data in their system and apply for multiple scholarships at one time. Going Merry also does a good job of including local scholarships, which are often easier to win than the larger well-known scholarships.

5. ScholarshipOwl - ScholarshipOwl.com aggregates different scholarships and organizes them by criteria like due date, award amount, requirements, and available awards. ScholarshipOwl will also automatically submit your application to scholarships that require your basic information.

6. Bold.org - Bold.org makes it easy for you to discover various scholarships you may qualify for, and you can screen by things like education level, category, amount, and deadline. You can also filter on scholarships that don't require an essay.

7. Cappex - Cappex.com holds itself out to be the largest online scholarship database. Similar to other providers, you will be required to create an account to see a list of scholarships you might be eligible for. Their site also allows you to find scholarships that provide funding for multiple years.

8. Scholly - Once you create your profile, MyScholly.com algorithms will search their database and create a list of scholarships you might be eligible for. Scholly creates a score for each scholarship, letting you know which scholarships are a better fit for you best on the data you provided. The higher your Scholly score, the better match you are for the scholarship.

9. CareerOneStop - The Department of Labor has a scholarship website you can access through their CareerOneStop.org portal. They have aggregated over 8,000 scholarships you can search by criteria like the amount, state, deadlines, etc. The site has scholarships for vocational school, associate programs, and undergraduate and graduate programs.

October

Get started familiarizing yourself with the FAFSA process. You can get the FASFA Worksheet at Fafsa.ed.gov. The FASFA process can be a bit confusing and complicated, so you want to start getting familiar with it now. The FAFSA form is typically available on October 1st for the following school year.

If you are applying to a private university or college, many will require financial aid applicants to fill out the CSS/Financial Aid profile along with your FAFSA.

Try to complete college admissions applications by the end of November, but make sure you review your target school's individual deadlines, especially if you are targeting early acceptance.

Get Organized Now

While national scholarships should not be ignored, ask your school guidance counselor about available local scholarships. Often companies make scholarships available for students in their local communities or for students of their employees. While researching your available options is certainly time-consuming and often frustrating, the effort can return large rewards for years to come. Begin applying for college scholarships now. This is one area you don't want to procrastinate.

Whether applying for national or local scholarships, preparing ahead of your applications ahead of time is an important first step. Start by compiling a list of both your academic and non-academic achievements. Next, you will want to create a summary of those achievements noting what you did, why it was important, and what you learned from the experiences. While this will take some thought and reflection on your part, it will serve as a great resource when working on your college and scholarship applications. Another reason you want to do this is to provide people who are writing letters of recommendation for you with additional material to write you an impactful letter. Here are the things you want to include:

- GPA (Grade Point Average) and scale used by your school. For instance, 3.85 out of a possible 4.

- Brief descriptions of any significant team and individual projects, research work, and papers.

- A list of the teams, clubs, groups, and organizations you participated in.

- List of awards, contests, and competitions.

- List your participation in volunteer and community work you've been involved with.

- Create an online and offline filing system for all your admissions, application, and financial aid documentation.

- Maintain a calendar with all of your applications, financial aid, scholarships, and college notifications dates.

- Make sure you review your calendar for any approaching deadlines weekly.

December

Before you start enjoying your winter break, this is a great time to review all your college deadlines and application status. You should confirm that your applications are complete or on schedule, as managing the many college timelines can be prone to errors and mistakes. Prioritize any tasks that can't wait until January.

February/March/April

College admissions letters will start arriving as early as February. Shortly after your admission letter, you will receive your financial aid award letter. Your award letter will describe for you the amounts and types of financial aid for which you have been awarded. The letter will also outline the cost of attendance along with your expected family contributions. Be sure to talk with the financial aid administrators at your college with any questions and potential additional options.

May

The 1st of May is commonly referred to as the National Candidate Reply Date. This is the date most colleges require their accepted students to make a decision on admissions and the financial award package.

When you let the college know that you will be attending, you will also accept or reject the financial aid award package. It is important to note that you do not have to accept each part of the financial aid package. Your school likely will require a non-refundable deposit to confirm your attendance.

Cost

Let's take a quick look at the big picture when it comes to the cost of college. The really expensive colleges in the United States charge more than $55,000 per year in tuition. Even less expensive public colleges and universities can put students and families in a financial bind. When considering cost, do not forget about fees, room and board, and transportation. Put together, these expenses can add thousands of dollars to your college costs.

Even if you are personally self-sufficient, keep in mind that the government will still consider the income and assets of your parents until you meet the criteria set by the federal government for independence. Family-based resources start with your family's current assets—including savings accounts, investments, and special funds devoted to college, such as 529 Education Plans.

These days, the typical family has not saved enough to pay for college. Studies of college savings habits show big gaps between what families have set aside, what they think they need and what they actually need. One growing strategy to deal with this gap is to attend a junior college that feeds into a 4-year college (feeder colleges). By knocking out your common core at a junior college, you can often save significant money and still obtain your college degree from that dream school.

While complete books are written on how to pay for college, the point I want to emphasize in this book is to make sure to not let the published cost of a school drive your decision. You should get a complete view of your individual financial aid packages prior to crossing any schools off your list based on the cost of attendance.

Location

When high school students ask themselves which college they should attend, what often comes to mind is just how far away they can get from home and still be able to get back for long weekends. They want to put some distance between their new life and their old life. They don't want Mom and Dad dropping by for those unannounced visits. Academic performance studies do show that performance declines on average when students are more than 250 miles from home. Each student is very different, so distance may or may not impact you. I can tell you that many students do eventually get the blues and miss home, so being able to get in the car and be home in a few hours can be a real mental health booster.

You should consider how a school's location can affect your college experience and personal growth. Will you enjoy a small town or a large city? Will the location match your lifestyle? Ask yourself just how far you want to move away from home. Some students are more comfortable with family close by, and others are ready to inject some distance.

Additionally, research a college's climate and geography. Both will influence the social activities you can engage in with your friends. Many colleges don't allow freshmen to bring a car to campus, so note how walkable the areas around campus are. Paying for transportation everywhere can get expensive quickly.

<u>Size of Universities and Classes</u>

According to the Carnegie Classification of Colleges and Universities, colleges considered "small" have fewer than 5,000 students. The "medium" category is classified between 5,000 to 15,000 students and large institutions exceed 15,000 students. The largest universities in the United States have well over 50,000 students. If you attended a small high school, attending that large state U with tens of thousands of students on campus and hundreds of students in some lecture halls can be overwhelming for some and exciting for others. Data does show that students who attended larger high schools make the transition smoother.

One of the biggest reasons cited by students when they transfer from large schools to smaller ones is that the students feel like a number. They missed personal interactions with their teachers and engaging dialogs in the classroom. Universities do work hard to overcome the class size challenges by creating small groups within each class and utilizing Teaching Assistants (TAs) to help build connections.

At a large school, you can still receive a more personalized educational experience if the college offers small class sizes. And even in classes with hundreds of students, teaching assistants will meet with small groups of students regularly to answer questions and provide individual assistance.

Class sizes reported by colleges are often significantly misleading as these statistics do not typically reflect the average student experience. The chart below was compiled by Kyle Giddon and published in his article entitled *"Why colleges average class size statistics are misleading."* Giddon explains that the actual student experience is often much different than the school's reported class size, but how can this be? To understand this, let's look at an exaggerated example. Let's say a college offers 5 sections of a course, and the class sizes are 1, 1, 1, 1, and 125. The average class size is 25.8, but 97% of students experienced a class size of 125. While these are extreme numbers to make a point, when you factor in Summer, Winter, and Night classes and unpopular majors, the numbers students experience in the classroom can vary greatly.

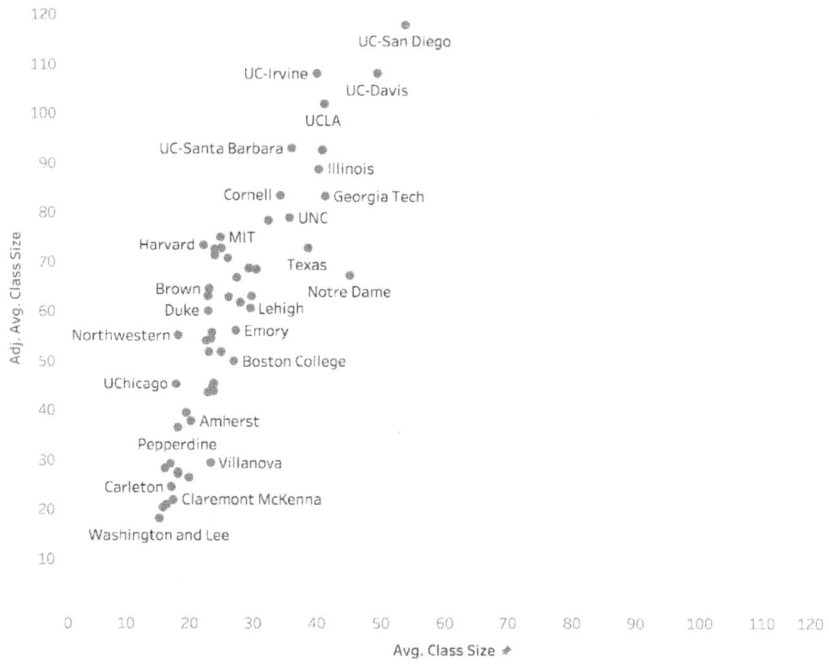

Source: Why colleges' "average class size" statistics are misleading and how to fix them - Kyle Giddon.

Giddon's data above shows the linear relationship between the average class size and the adjusted average class size. The college with the smallest class size, Washington and Lee University, had an average class size of 15.3 and an adjusted average of 18.3. On the other end of the spectrum was UC-San Diego, with an average class size of 53.7, moving to an adjusted class size average of 117.9. Giddon also computed the percentage change between each college's average class size and their adjusted average class size from the schools listed in the chart. He found that the adjusted class sizes were, on average, 116% greater, meaning that a typical student's average class size was actually more than double the reported average class size.

Academic Programs

One of the biggest frustrations for students entering college is that the "common core" of classes they take in their first year or two of college looks a lot like their high school class subjects. Many colleges do give students the opportunity to explore classes from different majors during their first year, so it might be a good idea to select a school that allows you to do that. This flexibility can give you insights as your interests will likely change over time. In fact, changing majors throughout college is incredibly common. The National Center for Education Statistics (NCES) data shows that about one-third of undergraduate students that had declared a major had changed their major at least one time. And one in ten students had changed their major more than once.

In addition to majors, many students will pursue a minor. When pursuing a minor, I like to recommend minors that will enhance the core skill set you are gaining in your major. For instance, a marketing major may want to minor in data analytics. A technology major may want to minor in business. If you decide to pursue a minor, make sure it will add value to your degree and not extend your graduation time. It is rarely worth extending graduation a semester or two just to pick up a minor.

Studying abroad programs can greatly enhance your college experience and subsequent marketability as a graduate. Many four-year colleges offer the opportunity to take a study abroad program at different times in your academic journey. Many colleges even have scholarship opportunities to allow students to participate economically in these opportunities. Make sure to research your major's opportunities on your college websites, as opportunities around study abroad qualifications, experiences, and costs do vary within each institution's individual college.

Accreditation

Accreditation matters. In the United States, accreditation most commonly refers to a regionally accredited university. There are six geographic regions for accreditation in the United States, and each has a non-governmental agency that oversees and accredits the degree-granting institutions headquartered in their region. There are six recognized regional accreditation boards:

- MSA - Middle States Association of Colleges & Schools
- NASC - Northwest Commission on Colleges & Universities
- NCA - North Central Association of Colleges & Schools
- NEASC - New England Association of Schools & Colleges
- SACS - Southern Association of Colleges & Schools
- WASC - Western Association of Schools & Colleges

Additionally, colleges have individual colleges within the school that may have their own accreditation. For instance, The Association to Advance Collegiate Schools of Business, also known as AACSB International, is an American professional organization that accredits Schools of Business.

Outside of accreditation, you can learn about a college's reputation by consulting ranking lists like US News and other reputable sources. These lists highlight schools by region, size, and specific majors.

It is important to understand that a school's reputation should only be one part of how to choose a college. The effort you put into your coursework will likely matter much more. For the vast majority of students, attending an accredited college will prepare them to launch a successful career upon graduation.

Quality of the Professors

The complexity of running a college or university continues to grow during a constantly evolving economic landscape. One way to manage costs for colleges is to expand the use of adjunct professors. Although these professionals possess a terminal degree and are usually expert practitioners, they generally receive a lower salary than tenured professors and usually teach a larger course load each semester.

While some will argue that overworked adjunct professors teaching your classes results in less individualized attention, I have found that to mostly not be the case. When the issue arises, it almost always is a result of an adjunct professor taking the position to help promote their business's stature in the community.

Students don't give much thought to how their choice of professor impacts their workload and GPA. Students may ask around a little, maybe look online at RateMyProfessors.com, but typically students are more concerned about their schedule than their professors. But not all professors are created equal.

Let's look at three different professors and see which professor you would choose?

Professor A - Has 6 years of experience and a lot of published articles in their field. They even did some widely referenced industry research and wrote an acclaimed book.

Professor B – Is a newly graduated Ph.D. professor with only one semester under their belt, no published articles, no widely cited research, and no books. We just don't know much about this professor.

Professor C – Has taught for 15 years, spent the last five as a dean, and has come back to teaching for the last couple of years. Has a great track record of teaching, service, and contributions to the university

Ok, who did you pick? Professor A, Professor C, few will pick Professor B. But, professor B, maybe your best choice!

I may be escorted out of the halls of every college for what I am about to tell you. Still, the reality is this is a general guideline, not a hard-fast rule, but it definitely applies more than you might think. You see, students believe they should be taking classes with long-term, accomplished, tenured faculty. Each semester, I put up these professor profiles and ask students who they would like to take a class with. The overwhelming majority pick the highly experienced faculty member. But why?

On the surface, it just makes good sense. I mean, who wants to take a course with an unknown new Ph.D. graduate or a first-semester professor with only a year or two of experience under their belt? But here is the real rub, you have to understand how the process of tenure works, and what tenure actually means.

Let's look at how you earn tenure at most universities. The formulas change, but let's look at the most popular method. Tenure is typically earned over the course of about 5 years, so if a professor is a Ph.D. and has been teaching for over 5 years, they likely have tenure. Tenure is typically earned based on three components:

1) Research,
2) Service to the University, and
3) Teaching effectiveness, i.e., student evaluations.

The hardest part of the formula for faculty is research. Research is competitive and time-consuming, and the peer review process before publishing is quite painful. Service to the university that's easy; it just takes up some time. Teaching, well, here is what is beat into young Ph.D.'s across the country, don't make it hard on yourself. Good grades lead to good reviews and make it easy for your students to give you good reviews. Focus on your research.

Now contrast this with a professor who has been teaching for over five years (you can bet they likely have tenure); they can't be fired unless they basically break the law or lose their academic standing. They have been overworked, likely doing two jobs for years so they can earn tenure. They are frustrated with years of student excuses, and did I mention they can't be fired unless they basically try hard to be fired!

Now from this new vantage point, which professor do you think you are more likely to have a better experience with? Which professor is likely more vested in your success? It is clear the deck is stacked in the non-tenure professors' favor. But what about that professor who came back from the Administration role? Don't they have a love for teaching as well? Don't they miss the student engagement, and that is why they are back teaching? Well, maybe! But the reality is most faculty can make more money in administration, the pay grades go up, and guess what, when they go back to teaching, they usually keep the same pay! What a nice way to coast into that state retirement plan.

Again, I am making broad statements here, and many faculty members are great, whether they are tenured or not. Still, just like in Vegas, where the odds favor the house, the odds favor the Ph.D. on the way to tenure, not already there.

But what if my professors don't have a Ph.D. or have a Ph.D. from a non-accredited school or an accredited school not recognized by my university accreditation body for the tenure track? These professors are classified as non-tenure track. Non-tenure track faculty are typically classified as either Teaching Associates, who are typically full-time, or Adjunct faculty, who can be full-time but typically are on a semester-to-semester renewal for their slot or position. Most Adjunct faculty are not focused on research, they are focused on teaching, and they have a passion for it. This focus on teaching often makes them very good at what they do and creates a great experience for students in the classroom.

Some universities do a great job hiring Adjunct professors, while others don't. It is a bit of a gamble. One thing I will say is to be careful of the Adjunct faculty members that are there to build their business. Take, for example, the accounting professor who really doesn't care about teaching but knows it looks great for business development that they teach accounting at the university. Teaching probably takes a back seat to their practice, and the student experience likely will suffer. Retired business leaders where teaching is a second career are typically among the highest-rated faculty members at universities.

These are all general guidelines for you. You want to take these guidelines into account. Still, you do want to talk to other students about their experiences. One of the benefits students receive from joining university clubs or organizations is access to students who have already gone down the road you are going. Their insights can be very valuable.

Of course, you can always check out RateMyProfessor.com and other online sources.

Also, pay close attention to the professor's introduction about themselves during the first day of class! Do they seem excited and enthusiastic, or are they just going through the motions?

Housing Options

Many universities let you apply for housing independent of your acceptance notification. Dorm selection is highly competitive, so apply as early as your school allows. The average cost for room and board is $11,950 for public institutions and $13,620 for private colleges for the most recent academic year, according to a report by College Data. Over the course of four years, living in a dorm could add more than $45,000 to your total cost of attendance.

A growing number of colleges are requiring first-year students to live on campus if they are not local. This policy is designed to connect students to campus life, and numerous studies show that living on campus your first year leads to better academic performance.

The cost of living varies greatly from city to city, and these costs can have a larger-than-expected impact on your total cost of attending college. Make sure to do your research, as all dormitories and dorm rooms are not created equal. Compare building ages, amenities, dorm room sizes, and location to your classes and the trade-off between how the college charges for the different housing options. Most students discover that off-campus housing costs less while offering a better lifestyle and moving off-campus once they qualify. If you are planning to join Greek Life, many colleges offer fraternity and sorority houses where members live together.

A quick note on meal plans. Most universities have several different meal plans, and students do find these extremely convenient and useful. You can usually get a significant discount by purchasing a complete-year plan but note that most plans are non-refundable.

Social Activities

Growing your relationships and social experiences is a significant part of college. Most large colleges have hundreds of clubs and organizations for you to participate in. Love D&D? There likely is a club for that. Want to trade stocks? There is likely a club for that. Frisbee golf, yup, there is likely a club for that. And if, for some reason, there isn't a club for a hobby or interest you, your school will have a well-defined process so you can get one started. If you enjoy your high school extracurricular activities, you should find out whether a college will allow you to pursue your passions.

A quick note on so-called "party schools" and their reputation. Many so-called party schools simply have a strict zero-tolerance policy and strongly enforce that policy. Still, others don't have a big social scene within walking distance of their campus, so their students are much more likely to party on campus. The point is, please don't disregard a school based on a headline number. You can find a good party on just about every college campus in this country if that is what you are looking for. How other students choose to spend their free time should not be the driving factor in your decision. Many so-called party schools offer excellent academic programs that can help you prepare for a successful career and life.

Diversity

Many students don't spend a lot of time thinking about diversity in their college selection process. A college with a diverse student body will provide you with valuable new experiences and perspectives. This is an even more important factor to consider if you grew up in a city where the majority of people were of the same racial, cultural, or socioeconomic background. Additionally, research whether your school enrolls mainly in-state or out-of-state students. How many international students make up the student population.

In addition to a college's overall diversity, explore the diversity of the surrounding community. Communities with a diverse population tend to offer a selection of cultural events, dining, entertainment, and other opportunities that can greatly enhance your college experience. Diversity can play a powerful role in your college experience, so don't ignore it in your selection process.

Accommodations and Resources

It is extremely important for students to get their accommodation in place prior to starting their first semester. Many schools will require revalidation of any high school 504 or similar plans. The process of getting your college accommodation plan in place can be time-consuming. Tackling your first semester without your needed accommodations can be stressful and overwhelming and is just not something you want to do. Accommodations are very common on the college campus, with 21% of undergraduate students having accommodations in place.

Larger institutions tend to have more resources in place to support students. It is no surprise to most to learn that the majority of students with disabilities are enrolled in a 4-year institution. Sixty-nine percent of students with disabilities choose 4-year colleges compared to 28 percent who went to 2-year colleges.

Even if you think you want to try to tackle your classes without your accommodations, it is always better to have your plan in place as a safety net. Your default mode should be to use your plan even if you don't need it. College can snowball on you, and your needs can quickly change. When it comes to accommodations, fight for each and every one.

Stress is a Fact of Life

College is a very stressful period of time for the vast majority of students. There are the pressures of exams, large amounts of reading, research papers, competition for grades, financial expenses, social pressures, and seemingly endless decisions about the future.

Recognize that the stress you are feeling is normal, and you are going to feel stressed with all that is going on in your life. You can easily start to feel like your life is spiraling out of control, but you're not alone, and your fellow students are feeling somewhat the same way. Mental health issues are quite common among college students. In fact, about half of college students had a psychiatric disorder in the past year, and 3 out of 4 students experienced some sort of mental health issue during college.

Consider the following:

- 85% of college students reported they had felt overwhelmed by what they had to do at some point in the past year.
- 42% of college students stated anxiety as the top concern.
- 30% of college students reported that stress had affected their academic performance.
- 25% of college students reported they were taking psychotropic medication.

In reality, the vast majority of students will need some form of support to succeed in college. Fortunately, most colleges offer support and counseling services at no additional fee. Make sure to research all your college's support systems and services, and not just those on the academic side.

Career Services

One of the most overlooked parts of the college selection process is the resources a university has available to support its students. One of the universal complaints among students facing graduation is that their college career services department is understaffed and overwhelmed. Most students just seem to think that once they graduate, they will have no issues finding that dream career with their newly minted degree in hand. The reality is a bit more sobering. The National Association of Colleges and Employers (NACE) reviewed the results for over a half million four-year college graduates. They looked at over 300 colleges and discovered that just a fraction over 50% of the recent class had landed a full-time job within six months of graduation.

Students who gain internship experience are 35% more likely to get a job offer after graduating than those students with no internships. So, researching college internship support is very critical to your future success. Ask directly what percentage of students receive internships during their time at this particular university? Of that percentage, what percentage of students earned an internship directly through the university? Ask how many university employees are 100% dedicated to fostering internship opportunities for students? How many employees are 100% dedicated to helping students with career services? It is not unusual for universities to have employees performing multiple roles, so it is important to know how many employees get up every day with the sole mission of helping you in your career success. If a university has 5 employees and 10,0000 students graduating each year, you can bet that you won't receive too much personal attention.

While starting your career may seem like another lifetime away, you really want to understand the career services that are available at your potential colleges.

In addition to university career services, alumni networks are extremely important to help college students attain a job. Some universities have very formal alumni networking opportunities both in person and online. While other universities may offer services through LinkedIn or other social media platforms.

Cover All Your Bases

Many of the top colleges in the United States have acceptance rates in the single digits. And the large schools in the top 100 rankings turn down a large percentage of applicants. Given the competitive nature of college admissions, most college counselors suggest you pick a reach school, a target or match school (two or three) where your academic credentials match those of the current incoming class, and a safety school. A reach school is a college with an acceptance rate below 30% and/or where your academic credentials are at the lower end or just below the school's average range of acceptance. A safety school is one where you have an 80% or higher chance of being accepted. When selecting a college, you really should be selecting a few colleges. It is important you research ways to increase your college admission chances and seek out college admission specialists who can help you increase your odds of finding admissions success with the schools of your choice.

Visit Campuses

Campus tours are an important part of the college selection process and can help you not just see the school but feel what it would be like to be on campus. It is important to note that many schools are in regions of the country that have extreme seasonal weather. If you are looking to attend a school that is located in a different region of the country than where you grew up, make sure to visit campus during those cold winters or hot summers.

It is really hard to differentiate one campus from another based on online photos and videos. When you visit the campus, you gain a real sense of campus culture during your tour. You get a feel for whether you could see yourself as part of the community.

While some schools allow potential students to sit in on classes, I don't really see that as a highly valuable experience. More times than not, students can feel intimidated by the experience, especially if they sit in on a large lecture hall class. If you want to sit in on a class, recognize that professors are vastly different, and your sample likely will not reflect your actual experience when enrolled.

Try to engage with random students during your tours. It is critical to remember that when you tour a college, the student guides are like well-trained salespeople. They are focused on selling the school. During the tour, be sure to view things with a critical eye and ask hard questions.

Try to avoid the basic questions about how they feel and if they are happy with the school. These students are very well-trained and will be overflowing with enthusiasm and excitement. I recommend asking the guide questions that require peeling the onion back a few layers. The following are a few questions to get you started:

- Do you have any friends or acquaintances that transferred to other colleges?
- Why do you think most students transfer to other colleges when they leave here?
- What are a few things they know now; that they wish they knew as a first-year student?
- What were the hardest adjustments for them?
- If they could change one or two things about campus, what would it be? Usually, you will get parking as an answer. Try to dig a little deeper.
- How long does it typically take to get a meeting with a professor when you have a question? Many will say you have to meet with a Teaching Assistant first.
- What do they think about the meal plans on campus? It is reported that the meals you get during the campus tour are not the typical meals you get week to week. Ask students around campus to get the real skinny. In most cases, meal plans are well worth the investment in your first year.
- Are most classes taught by professors or teaching assistants?
- Have you had an internship off campus?
- Are internships easy to find through the school's career services department?
- Why did you choose this school?
- What other schools did you consider?

- Are there any summer reading requirements or training needed prior to arrival? Often colleges will require training on safety, security, and drugs and alcohol.

Make sure to put together your list of questions before you visit campus. Do not be afraid to ask questions on your tour. If others are visiting campus with you, you can pass out questions to them as well. Asking questions is critical, so don't be shy.

Special Considerations For Athletes

One of the biggest challenges many high school students face is the decision of whether they want to keep playing their favorite high school sport in college. For many students, this means forgoing a Division 1 (D1) college education for a D2 or D3 college education. Many students don't realize that many D1 schools have club sports programs that are on par with many D2 and D3 collegiate programs. How to prioritize your sport is a highly personalized decision, but just make sure that you research all your potential options before deciding.

Top Mistakes to Avoid in Choosing a College

First, let me put you at rest. You likely can have a great college experience at hundreds of colleges, not just one or two. Don't try to over-optimize your decision. Selecting a college and waiting on that acceptance letter is a very stressful process for many. It is important for us to not just discuss what we should do but we need to look at common mistakes that lead to suboptimal decisions in the college selection process.

1. Procrastination.

Finding a college that fits takes some time and effort. There is not just the research process but the often time-consuming and lengthy application process. Putting things off is not a good idea. When you take the time to reflect and think about the process, you will experience less stress and will be much more confident in your decision.

2. Birds of a feather.

Too many people choose a college because their best friends chose a particular school, or maybe the person they have been dating chose a school. While this sounds like a great idea at the time, college is one of the most pivotal decisions at this point in your life. Do you really want to make such a significant decision based on your current relationships? Remember that strong, healthy relationships can endure distance.

3. The gravity of legacy.

There can be a lot of pressure on students to follow in their family member's footsteps. This pressure can feel like the weight of gravity pulling you away from any other college choice. It is important you do your own research, explore different opportunities, and have thoughtful conversations about why a particular college works for you. The initial disappointment any family member may have will be gone once they see you thriving.

4. Having a high school degree will travel.

Some students just want to get away from home so bad that they will completely ignore colleges that are close to home. For some, this is the right decision, but for others, they could have gotten a great education and the independence they desired closer to home. Make sure to not make your college decision based on spite or an overwhelming belief that the further away from home, the better. Life happens. People get sick, stressed out, injured, and even die. The distance from home could make the difference between a very difficult situation and an impossible situation. Choose based on what you want, not what you want to avoid.

5. You're a big sports fan.

Too many students choose a college because they grew up a big fan of a sports program there. Look, if you're not playing on the team, being a fan of the sports program is not likely something that will connect directly with your academic programs. You can be a fan anywhere in the world, but not all colleges with great sports programs will be a great fit for you. Many students' identities are tied to a football program, for instance. The thoughts of tailgating with friends before games and being a part of that culture are of significant importance. I understand that. Let that connection tip the scales, not be the scale.

6. Extracurriculars.

Too many students choose a school because it is close to the beach, ski resorts, hiking trails, or great nightlife. Unless you plan to be a professional athlete or partygoer, extracurricular activities should complement your college selection decision, not drive it. Most all colleges have an abundance of activities and clubs on campus. These activities are a crucial part of your college experience, but they should not be the most important part.

7. Assuming you're not worthy.

Many students believe a school is just out of reach, just too costly, or maybe even just too difficult. Please don't overly self-regulate in your initial selection process. You never know how much you can achieve until you try. Personal growth happens outside your comfort zone, so embrace the possibilities.

8. Believing a particular college is too expensive.

If you recall from our earlier discussion, your expected family contribution (EFC) is based on family income, the net value of assets, the number of children in college, and family size. Financial aid packages are a combination of various forms of student aid (grants, scholarships, loans, and employment) offered by a college and other sources to meet a student's financial needs. You really want to see the process through before ruling out a school based on the published price of attendance. You can also seek more financial aid from a school. Reach out and let them know how excited you are to attend but tell them you need a little more financial help. Many colleges have additional resources in these situations.

9. Saving costs on the scouting trips.

Visiting schools can get expensive, and many students' budgets are already taxed. It is important that you make every effort to visit and tour your potential schools. You want to experience campus for yourself, and level set your expectations. While others may have given the college rave reviews, it's always better to explore the campus and surrounding community for yourself if at all possible.

10. Ranking up.

Some students just selected the highest-rank school they got into. They love the idea of the prestige of the school. Don't assume that just because a school is highly ranked, it's the best fit for you. As Malcolm Gladwell said, sometimes it is better to be a big fish in a small pond.

11. Assuming parents or others know the best.

Don't assume somebody else knows better than you. Sure, others could have a lot of good insights, and you will want to take those all into the equation. But it is really important for you to think about what you want out of your college experience.

12. The train left the station years ago.

Many students have had their eyes on a particular college from a very young age. Maybe somebody they looked up to went there. They thought the college mascot was cool or for any other host of reasons. Don't get fixated on one school and decide to not check out others. You can still attend that long-held dream school, but often when you look, you find a better dream.

13. Letting a major drive your decision.

The major you have your eyes on might not be the major you stick with. A significant number of students switch majors, so it is best to build a little optionality into your decision. A college that offers you a variety of fields of study can go a long way as you discover more about yourself at the world in general.

Thinking about college as an investment in yourself and your future can help you focus on your college selection process. You want to commit to being the best version of yourself and taking full advantage of the opportunity in front of you.

Your purpose and your why become the guiding lens that will focus and enhance your college selection, career, and life. Purpose and your underlying why isn't something you just make up on the fly. Your purpose is something that you discover. Doing the exercises in this book will help you along on your journey, ensuring you consider significant and meaningful things throughout your life. These exercises are very effective in helping determine your purpose.

After all, applying your talents to something that is bigger than you and making an impact in a way that matters to you is a truly fulfilling way to live. To do that, we need to identify what we care about. Doing this is a crucial first step to help you start your college journey with real clarity.

I Am Not Happy. Should I Transfer Colleges?

The decision to transfer colleges is certainly not one to be taken lightly. Before transferring, make sure you have all your credits approved prior to paying your tuition. Once you are paid up, you will likely find it a bit more difficult to get all your credits transferred in.

Quite a few students are not happy with their decision to transfer, and some even experience what people call "transfer shock." Students often discover that the grass is not always greener on the other side.

However, the vast majority of students who transfer have a positive experience and earn their degrees. I personally had a student in one of my classes who attended three prior colleges. She had finally found her home with her fourth college, and she was finally thriving. So, if your first couple of schools don't work out, don't give up. Keep looking.

Before you commit to transferring colleges, you want to make sure you are transferring for the right reasons. Hers are a few questions to ask to help you with that decision:

- Does transferring to college make sense financially?
- Does the new college provide a truly different environment?
- How will the change affect my academic standing and future performance?
- How will transferring impact your graduation date?
- How will transferring colleges impact career opportunities?

One smart strategy is transferring from a two-year school to a four-year institution. Most of the top companies are looking for students with bachelor's degrees who can advance up the ranks. A recent CareerBuilder survey found that 38% of employers raised their educational requirements for job positions over the last five years.

Transferring colleges due to financial or family reasons is often a prudent choice as well. Remember to apply for financial aid and make sure you understand the impact on any existing scholarships or financial aid package you currently have.

Often students consider transferring schools because they don't feel their current school is a good fit. If you are feeling that way, it is a good idea to journal about what you are experiencing. Often times students find out, they are simply stressed out or feeling a bit overwhelmed. By seeking the help of campus counselors, they often find that their reasons for wanting to transfer were the results of normal college transition issues and not the college itself.

Many students struggle initially adjusting to college academics. If academic concerns are driving your decision to want to transfer, you may want to make sure you are utilizing all available resources you have on campus. Transferring with a low GPA can be difficult, and you may have trouble finding a college you will be happy with. Often it is worth the effort to buckle down, get help, and improve your grades.

Deciding to transfer colleges is no small decision. Before making that final decision to transfer, make sure you are not being driven by your emotions. Make sure to take your time and do your research. You will want to take a trip and spend some time on the campus of the college you're considering transferring to. While on campus, you should make an effort to talk with students, staff, faculty, and advisors in the college major department you want to join. By taking the time to meet the people you will be spending your time with, you can make sure if you do transfer schools, you do, in fact, improve your situation. Sometimes the grass at your new school isn't any greener than that of the school you are leaving or left.

Why Do Students Transfer Colleges?

Transferring colleges is a very common experience for students, so don't feel like you are alone in thinking about transferring. Even students who make a seemingly great decision learn, grow, and find new things that excite them. My own kid went off to a top university as he wanted to work with NASA. While there, he fell in love with cyber security and decided to transfer to colleges to pursue that vision. As I write this paragraph, he is celebrating his two-year anniversary as a cybersecurity engineer. Sometimes on the path to your dreams, you stumble upon another path that excites you even more. With that said, let's look at some of the most common reasons that students report as the reason for their transfers.

Wrong Environment

For many students, the change from a relatively small high school campus to a large college environment can be more than a bit overwhelming. For many, things seemed much different during their freshman orientation, when everything was organized, followed a schedule, and there was someone there to help everywhere they turned.

They Feel Socially Isolated

Many students find themselves away from family and friends, and they start to miss those strong connections. They see their friends on social media having a great time at their local college, and that makes them feel even more socially isolated at their own school. It is a natural part of the college experience to feel homesick or find yourself missing others who are significant to them more than they expected. I even had a student who transferred because he could stand being away from the family dog. Given time, most students naturally adjust to their new environment, and before long, they post photos on social media with their new friends, having the time of their lives.

Changing Majors

National Center for Education Statistics shows that 30% of undergraduates changed their major at least one time. And in a Best Colleges survey, 61% of college graduates said that if they had another opportunity, they would change their major. The fact is that when many students decide to change their major, they often transfer to schools where they can pursue a better fit for their new major.

School Recognition and Prestige

We all know that certain colleges hold more prestige than others. These prestige colleges look great on resumes, have influential alumni, and can be a ticket to a fast start on the career track of choice. Some students who did not perform their best in high school will choose a college with the intention of establishing a solid GPA for a year or two and then apply to transfer to a more prestigious school. This is a solid strategy for students who underperform to their capabilities in high school.

Poor Academic Performance

Students' poor academic performance often drives a desire for a fresh start. They might have stretched themselves a little too far with their initial college selection. They might have found themselves in an environment where they had no time for anything but academics. A new school will likely lead to a better overall college experience.

Financial Situation

Attending a four-year college can be very expensive. Increases in housing, tuition, living expenses, and financial challenges can all cause students to reevaluate their college choice. Experiencing piles of debt can be overwhelming and feel completely different than the expectation seemed during the college selection process.

Many students experience online courses, adjunct faculty, and seemingly endless teaching assistants and start to feel that the level of education they're receiving isn't in line with the cost they're paying. Many students who transfer for financial reasons transfer back to an in-state or community college where they can take advantage of lower tuition and living costs.

Sports Transfer

For quite a few student-athletes, the college experience differed greatly from what they were pitched. Perhaps they aren't getting the playing time they were promised. Maybe a coach that recruited them left or was let go. Maybe they aren't getting along with their teammates or coaches. Maybe they lost their scholarship, suffered an injury, or are having problems academically. The fact is things can change, expectations can shift, new opportunities may arise. All this adds another layer of complexity for student-athletes.

Job Transfer

It is much more common for college students to maintain a full-time job while they pursue their college degrees. Many colleges now offer online, and hybrid undergraduate and graduate programs designed to accommodate full-time working professionals. When working students transfer or start new jobs in another city or state, they may often need to transfer to another college to stick to their intended graduation plan.

Picking A Major That Fits

Let Me Put You Right At Ease

For many students, picking a major seems like a life-or-death decision! Many students just pick a major because they have gotten tired of well-meaning people continually asking them about it. Let me put you right at ease here, according to a recent study, only 27% of people end up working in a job closely related to their major. About 30 to 50 percent of students in the United States end up changing their major at least once. So, take a deep breath and know you have time on your side.

The reality is, at 17 or 18 years old, how could you possibly be expected to know what you want to do for the rest of your life? With all that said, let's dive deeper into the whole major topic.

Applying with a Declared Major or Undecided?

If you're applying undeclared because you're unsure about what you want to study, that is perfectly fine! Studies have shown that applying to college undeclared does not have a negative impact on a student's chances of being admitted.

However, if you do know what you want to study, applying undeclared is not generally a good strategy. The idea of applying without declaring a major is that you have time to explore and try different areas of study. However, this is not without some downsides. The downside is that you will not be able to take advantage of some major-specific classes, mentorship programs, outside activities, or internship opportunities that are available to those students that have declared their major.

At most universities, you're not guaranteed a spot in your desired major unless you actually applied and were accepted under that major. The process of changing majors can be difficult. Some schools have a separate process for students wanting to change majors. If your major is especially competitive, the process might be extremely bureaucratic and difficult.

If you have a competitive major you want to apply for, but your high school performance may not be up to par, you can use the first year of college to build a strong GPA. In this case, it might make sense to apply as an undeclared student.

There are some situations in which it may benefit you to declare your major on your college application. If your major requires a specific curriculum starting in your freshman year, then it is certainly in your best interests to declare your major.

Applying to college with a specific major may also allow you to qualify for additional financial aid such as department-specific scholarships, special freshman housing, or professional development opportunities that are only available to declared students. The bottom line is this, take a look at your individual situation and your universities policies, and make the decision that works best for your needs.

Declaring A Major

Declaring a major is a rite of passage in college. You will eventually need to declare a major, typically before you start your junior year. The time to make your major decision will come quicker than you think, but you do have two solid years to explore your options.

Students yet to declare a major can still enter their junior year, but classes at this level are major-specific, and you will likely be adding additional semesters to your college career if you have not decided on your major.

I always recommend that students declare a major by junior year, even if they are still uncertain. Remember, only 27% of people end up working in a job closely related to their major, so take your best guess and just get on with it.

Six Core Categories Of Majors

Choosing a college major was difficult enough back in your parent's day when there was only a handful of majors for them to choose from. Today, there are hundreds of majors you can choose from.

The good news is it is not as complex as it may first appear. All these hundreds of different college majors typically fall into six categories. At first glance, it could seem to be an impossible task to sort through hundreds of different possibilities but don't panic. By focusing on six general categories, you can narrow down your search. Let's look at the core six:

- Arts-Related Majors
- Business-Related Majors
- Environment-Related Majors
- Engineering and Technology Majors
- Science and Math-Related Majors
- Literature, Language, and Social Science Majors

Sometimes, we know more about what we don't want as opposed to what we do want. Hate math, don't have an artistic bone in your body, well, you just eliminate two of the six categories. Sometimes by eliminating the things we don't like; we can narrow our options down to discover the things we will like. So, the first step is to eliminate the categories that you have little to no interest in.

Next, identify which of the general categories pique your interest. Do you enjoy social media? Are you creative, and do you enjoy helping people share their messages? A major in Digital Marketing may make all the sense in the world for you. Do you like numbers, and enjoy creating and building things? Maybe architecture is your path. Love investing and the stock market, helping people achieve their financial goals, maybe wealth management is in your future.

I am amazed at the number of students who pick a major that they have no real aptitude for. They picked their major because the job outlook was good, they heard they could make good money in the field, or maybe following in the footsteps of their parents. **Please don't do that!** Take the time to explore different options.

Take Some Time

Take the time you need to try out some different classes and gain new experiences, and you will be in a good position to make your decision. Success is most often found at the intersection of your talents and your passions.

Take the time to find your passion. When you choose a college major, you are choosing the initial direction you will be launching your career. You might even follow that path for a big part of your career. That's why it's important to find something you are passionate about.

I recommend students take an elective class that is outside their comfort zone. This approach will help you dive into areas you never knew you might enjoy but could end up being exactly what gets you excited.

Of course, you'll also want to consider other factors that will have an impact on your future. Many folks are burdened financially and, must realistically, balance their passions with the practical realities of paying the bills.

Unfortunately, I see so many students give up on their dreams at 17, 18, or 19 years old! It really does break my heart. I hear things like, "I wanted to be a nurse, a doctor, an engineer, but those majors are just too hard." Too hard! Just wait until you experience your future for a decade or two. You will learn the meaning of hard!

Too many students are under the false impression that all college degrees are created equal, that GPA really doesn't matter, and that any college degree will put them on the golden path to massive success.

Now is the time in your life to challenge yourself, grow, work hard, and make sacrifices, so you can benefit from all your hard work for the rest of your life. Success has a compounding effect, just like earning interest on your money. Do the hard work now, so things will be easier in the future. If you goof off at this point in your life, you will face decades of hard consequences. Challenge yourself now, test yourself, and find out just how good you can be!

Does My Major Need More Work?

Some majors require an advanced degree to significantly increase your odds of getting a job and having a fulfilling career. Majoring in psychology? You most likely will need a master's degree or Ph.D. to pursue many of the most rewarding positions. Studying Economics? You likely will need a Ph.D. for the majority of the jobs in that field. Studying Management? Well, you will be competing with those who have years of work experience as well as others with MBAs.

One exercise I make my students do is to pretend they are graduating in 30 days and find 7 to 10 jobs they would be interested in applying for and look to see what the requirements are for those jobs.

Take those jobs and identify the skills gap you have, and work to close that gap as you head toward graduation. Do all the jobs you like require a master's degree? Do the jobs you like require a specific technical skill like SQL? Do they require internship experience? Certain certifications? The key is to develop a roadmap so when graduation does come, you are in the best position to launch your career.

One of the best ways to determine if a particular major is for you is to talk to other students in that major already. Learn why they picked their major and what they like and dislike about their majors. Ask them what things they wish they had known back when they were freshmen.

Ask them about their internships, clubs they participated in, professors they really liked, and, well, the professors they didn't care for too much. Ask them to describe the challenges and opportunities. By talking to students who are already well down the path you are considering, you can gain valuable insights and knowledge.

Do I Need A Minor?

What is a minor? Think of it like a mini-major. Minors are obtained by focusing your optional classes on a specific track or minor (usually four to six upper-level classes). One of the frequent questions I get is… "Should I Pick Up a Minor?" My answer to this question ranges from YES to NO, to MAYBE. The first question I ask is… "What are you trying to accomplish by picking up a minor? You need to make sure you have a clear vision of how a minor will help you achieve your goals.

Sometimes, you can pick up a minor without having to pick up any additional classes. If you plan far enough ahead, fitting a minor into your schedule while meeting your core requirements is entirely possible.

However, in many cases, a minor is just more effort and cost than it's really worth. Rarely is adding a minor worth extending your graduation another semester. Taking on the challenge of a minor can be very useful if it complements your major. Say you're a digital marketing major, and you pick up a minor in data analytics. A big part of marketing is analytics. A minor in data analytics can give you an edge. Maybe you're a computer science major, and a minor in business could help you show that not only can you code, but you have an understanding of business as well. A minor can show that you are strategic, determined, and take the initiative.

A minor won't cover up shortcomings in your academic performance, and many hiring managers will not place much weight on your minor versus your major, so if you are going to tackle a minor, make sure you are taking it on for the right reasons.

The Big Picture

Recent research shows that 62% of college graduates are working in a job that requires a degree. However, only 27% of college graduates are working in a job that closely relates to their college major. I don't want to totally downplay or disregard the impact of a major on your future earnings potential. There is no question that certain majors pay significantly more than other majors. I am just saying that your major doesn't have to pigeonhole you into a particular job or field for life.

There are definitely majors that pay more than others. For instance, a recent survey showed that Counseling Psychology majors make an average of $29,000 per year, compared to $120,000 for Petroleum Engineering majors. That's a difference of 314 percent—or $4.1 million over a 45-year lifetime of work.

Another example is the difference between two popular majors, General Business and Elementary Education. A General Business major earns $60,000 annually, compared with $40,000 for an Education major. Over a lifetime, that's a difference in earnings of about $900,000.

If you want to be an accountant, architect, engineer, doctor, attorney, etc., your major can obviously have a significant impact on your ability to pursue those professions. But as your career develops, your experience is what people will be evaluating. Too many students just don't take advantage of the opportunities they have in college to network, get involved in student organizations, and volunteer for causes they are passionate about. These types of activities reflect well on your resume; they tell employers that you are passionate, motivated, and focused.

So, to get going, pick one of the six categories of majors and listen to a lot of podcasts in that area. Say you like the idea of a business-related major, but you have no real idea what you want to do in the field of business. Head over to iTunes and find the top-ranked podcasts in business. Listen to podcasts on marketing, management, leadership, entrepreneurship, economics, and so on, find a topic that resonates with you, then dig deeper… read some books, blog posts, and research papers on the topic, and see if you are still interested. Listening to podcasts, watching YouTube Videos, Ted Talks, etc., are all great ways to uncover your passions and interests you never knew you had and, ultimately, a major and career that you are excited about.

Finding A Career That Fits

The network you build in college may matter way more than your college major. According to HubSpot, 85% of jobs are filled through networking. In fact, according to CNBC, 70% of jobs are never published publicly.

The vast majority of students head off to college because they believe it will lead them to their best future. And one of the keys to making that dream a reality is to focus on building a network that will help you launch your dream career and future. And while it has been said it is not what you know but who you know, the reality is both are extremely important. Too many students just focus on their academics and close circle of family and friends. These students don't put much effort into building their professional network. Please don't be one of those students. Make building your professional network a priority from day one.

Build Your Network

LinkedIn's research also confirms that most jobs are found through personal connections – 70% of them, to be exact!

Networking is truly critical to those who want to be successful, and you should make a significant investment of time and energy into networking during your college career. Networking should be on par with the efforts you put into your academic studies. The reality is that you are much more likely to get a job through your network than through the university career center. This is not a knock-on university career centers; it's just a pure numbers game. With thousands of students to serve, you can't rely on your university to find you that dream job. They have lots of resources to help you, they may even lend you the car, but it is up to you to do the driving.

You should start networking as soon as you hit campus. Start by building relationships with your professors, academic advisors, and other students in your dorm and classrooms. Setting a weekly goal of new connections to create on LinkedIn is one of the best strategies you can employ. Your network can be a very important source of mentorship and play a pivotal role in helping you discover your major, not to mention a source for internships and career opportunities. Networking is all about actual engagement - creating relationships, interacting with professionals who share your passion, building your following, and connecting with people.

According to a study done by LinkedIn, 35% of participants said a casual conversation through LinkedIn Messaging led to a new opportunity. And 61% of participants believe that regular online interaction with their network can lead to possible job opportunities.

Building a strong network can benefit your career and future. Too many people approach networking as a one-way street. Make sure to maintain a balance between giving and taking during your networking efforts. The most successful networkers give more than they take. They make introductions, connect people, and always seem to find a way to create value for others. While there are a lot of networking sites, LinkedIn is the undisputed heavyweight champ. Beyond simply networking, you can use LinkedIn to share ideas, seek feedback, and increase your professional credibility. Let's explore LinkedIn and how it can help you achieve your future goals.

Genuine Relationships

Even though LinkedIn is an online platform, it allows for the building of genuine relationships. By allowing the building of relationships through multiple levels of connections, your connections can make personal associations, garner feedback, seek advice, and even provide valuable mentorship. These connections and relationships you build can help you find job leads, referrals, and much more.

Expanded Reach

LinkedIn lets you connect with the billions of people all over the world who are online every day – how else could you meet these folks? But one of the best ways to connect with folks is through your meetings at career fairs, trade shows, community events, and so on.

Grow Your Brand

LinkedIn is a great place to post your schoolwork, share your ideas, and enhance your professional reputation. When people research you online, a well-built LinkedIn profile will help you control how people see your brand. LinkedIn also gives you the opportunity to meet future employers, business partners, suppliers, clients, staff, and friends.

Fresh Perspectives & Insights

Through things like LinkedIn groups, people's posts, etc., you get access to the latest business trends and what's happening in your field. LinkedIn allows you to engage directly with future colleagues in your field, follow their interests, and learn their thoughts and opinions on industry topics.

Establish a Process

Put together a plan to continually find new contacts and to continue to build relationships with existing ones. The best part about regularly checking in with your contacts is that when you do need a favor, it comes from a natural place, not just seen as an 'ask.'

Start by identifying the process you'll use to continue your networking efforts. One easy process is to create a weekly event on your calendar that reminds you to network.

If you plan to directly network with specific people, add about ten names of the people that you want to connect with, whether new or existing. Make sure you include a note for yourself about who they are and your reason for wanting to connect. If there is someone you want to connect with on a regular basis, create a recurring event solely for that person.

If you're networking indirectly or in groups, remember that the people who are most effective visit their top groups daily and look for questions they can answer. One of the big benefits of networking through social media is that it doesn't take a lot of time, and you can do it whenever you have free time.

Don't forget, while following a system is helpful, there are times that you may want to spontaneously reach out, and that's okay too.

Success Tip: You should use a spreadsheet to keep track of your interactions, not just for relationship-building tracking but also so that you have that information outside of the social media platform. It makes it easier to see the status of relationships at a glance, and it ensures you don't lose the data if a particular social media network were to shut down or close your account.

Some ways in which you can indirectly network are to:

- Join and participate in groups frequented by the people you want to connect with.
- Follow pages and influencers to learn more about different industries and get more insight into your ideal customer.
- Post questions to gather feedback and start discussions.
- Contribute to discussions by commenting on other posts.
- Post your original content to expand your reputation as an expert.
- Share content regularly to solicit likes, opinions, feedback, and more.
- Become a customer by following different company pages to gain insights.

Success Keys:

- List 2-3 of your professional networking goals as they relate to your future career goals (e.g., get a consistent source of internship leads, increase your visibility, grow your network, etc.).
- Outline specifically what you want to achieve (e.g., build relationships with people from XYZ industry, connect with X number of people, build X number of relationships with industry influencers, find potential employers/jobs, grow a support network for sharing information/tips/resources, etc.).
- Set a time frame for each stage of your goal. For example, make xx number of connections by xx date).

Growing Your Network

“Your network is your net worth. How do you value your network? Well, if you don’t value it, cultivate it, nurture it, it becomes worthless. If you do value it, it becomes priceless.” - Robert G. Allen.

Reflect on Your Process. Take time to reflect and check in with how your social media networking is going. Evaluate the system you’ve put in place, and ask yourself: “What have you been doing that has worked in connecting with new people? What hasn’t?”

Seek New Opportunities. Look for opportunities to meet with online contacts in person to further relationships. And in reverse, make sure that whenever you meet new people offline, you reach out to connect with them on LinkedIn too. Always send a quick “thank you” to new connections.

Routinely Touch Base. Develop a consistent process of following up through email, message, or telephone to nurture relationships. You’ll soon get a feel for the sweet spot for reaching out – too little, and you’ll risk being forgotten. Too much, and you could start to be annoying. It’s also okay if you don’t want to nurture all relationships; sometimes, you just don’t click with someone.

Be Natural. Networking should be natural, not forced. Keep it simple, and don’t overcomplicate things. It’s okay to send a simple hello and let people know you are thinking about them. Reach out during holidays, birthdays, work anniversaries, and other occasions, good or bad.

Be Inclusive. Grow your network by including your connections in events you’re attending, whether in-person or online. You can also add them to a group you host. This makes it easy for you to find common ground and create regular engagement by knowing what they’re up to. The golden rule with LinkedIn or any social media networking is to “use good judgment.” This means that you want to provide more value than you take, be respectful and appropriate, and always put your best foot forward.

Networking is an effective way to make new connections and nurture existing connections. Too many students wait until their senior year before they shift their focus from their academics to their network. Perhaps the most important takeaway is that it's important to have a strong network in place well before you need it.

The facts are overwhelming. Most people find their jobs through their networking efforts. And a large number of sales and business leads happen as a result of networking efforts. Despite all the benefits of networking, according to research by HubSpot, one in four professionals don't network at all. Based on my personal experience, the number of students not networking is much greater. Please don't be one of those people sitting on the sidelines. Networking is essential for identifying potential internships, job opportunities, and continued future career success.

Informational Interviews

Informational interviews are not about finding a job but about gathering information and building relationships. It is critical to your future career success that you use informational interviews to connect with people working in the field that interests you. Reaching out to individuals on LinkedIn whose jobs seem interesting to you is a great place to start. Let them know who you are and if you're looking to talk to them about their career and industry. Most successful people are more than happy to help students on their journey. Let's look at a few of the key benefits of conducting informational interviews:

- They allow you to bridge the gap between your class lessons and what it is actually like to work in the field.
- They allow you to gain insights into how well-aligned a potential career is with your skills, talents, interests, and passions.
- They allow you to identify the gaps between your academic program and the skills employers are looking for in the marketplace.
- They take your networking to the next level by giving your personal relationships into the hidden job market, where 80% of jobs are actually filled.

- They provide you valuable career planning insights.
- They allow you to gain experience and confidence interacting with professionals in the marketplace.
- They are amazing sources of professional networking referrals.

When conducting informational interviews, we want to focus on five key components to get the most out of each informational interview.

1. Foundation – LinkedIn Profile, Resume, Letter of Interest, and Elevator Pitch.
2. Research – Industry, Company, Person.
3. Preparation – Modality, Questions, Flow.
4. Three Phases – Introduction & Small Talk, Q&A, and Closing.
5. Follow up – Post Interview, Regular Cadence.

Foundation

The foundational tools for your informational interviews are the same fundamental tools you will need for your job search. These include a well-designed LinkedIn profile, resume, letter of Interest, and elevator pitch. Let's look at each one of these components individually.

LinkedIn is like your resume that never sleeps. When building your profile, use a professional photo. Don't use a photo of your dog, a group photo, etc. You want to use a professional headshot. Many universities make professional photographers available for their students. You can check with your first-year experience professor or career center to discover what resources are available to you.

Next, you want to make sure you have a great headline. You want to tell people what you are excited about and what you want to achieve. For example, a Finance Major and Aspiring Wealth Manager or a Marketing Major and Aspiring Social Media Manager.

After you have completed your headline, you want to write an effective summary. You want to describe what motivates you, what you are passionate about, and what skills you have developed. You want to review job descriptions you are interested in and use those skill requirements to help develop your summary. Don't keyword stuff here. You want to make sure you naturally work those skills into your summary in a way that demonstrates your personality.

Next, we want to go to work on adding your experience to your profile. List the jobs you have had, including part-time. From a chronological perspective, you want to start with your most current work experience and go backward. List your key accomplishments and skills you developed during each position.

After that, you want to list the organizations you have participated in along with your responsibilities and duties. Make sure to outline what the organization is about and the organization's purpose or mission.

Following your organization section is your education. You will start with your most recent college. List your major, GPA, awards, scholarships, etc. Include any of your summer programs or study abroad classes you have taken.

Volunteer work is often overlooked, but you want to be sure to include your volunteer experience. Treat this section just like your experience section. Many hiring managers and Human Resource personnel put volunteer experience on par with work experience.

Skills and Expertise is up next. Again, you want to utilize those skills identified in the job descriptions you were attracted to. You want to include at least five skills here. This will serve as a base for your connections to recommend you for those skills.

Make sure to list any honors and awards you have earned. List key classes that support your career goals. If you have worked on any projects that helped you develop valuable skills, make sure to include those in your profile.

Finally, you want to ask your professors, supervisors, mentors, etc., to write recommendations for you. Make sure the person you are asking for a recommendation from can honestly speak to a particular skill.

Your Resume

A well-written resume is a requirement for any student looking to launch a great career. And while different companies place different levels of importance on the resume, it is a universally accepted screening tool for human resource executives across the globe.

A well-written resume is concise, free of grammatical errors, and gives a good overview of your achievements and experiences; and should communicate you are the type of employee the hiring company is seeking.

As a college student seeking an internship or first career, potential employers are well aware you don't have a long work history and lots of industry experience. What they are most concerned about is your work ethic, willingness to learn, maturity level, ambitions, and work ethic. The focus of your resume is to show how college, high school, and activities have helped you develop these traits.

While as a student, you have not accumulated decades of career experience, there are many skills that you have developed. You can use these skills to bridge the gap in your new career. Maybe the position you seek is looking for strong leadership skills. Were you a team captain in high school? Did you lead a school fundraiser? Were you a team leader at church camp? Most students have served in a leadership role at some point, so your job is to show how those skills translate to that dream job.

When looking for areas in your past to demonstrate common job requirements like being a team player, taking criticism well, building teams, having great communication skills, etc., look to your past activities. Things like church work, summer camp activities, sports, volunteer work, travel, part-time work, etc., can all be used to demonstrate skills you have developed.

While everyone has different opinions and ideas about building resumes, here are the core sections you should include:

1. Contact information
2. Education/Objective
3. Work experience
4. Key skills as they relate to the job description
5. Memberships and Activities
6. Interests & Hobbies

1. Contact Information

The goal of this section is to include the basic information needed so a company representative can quickly contact you. I highly recommend you spend the time building out your LinkedIn profile and including your profile link URL in this section. In this section, you should include the following:

Your First and last name, address, phone number, email, and LinkedIn profile URL. If you are moving due to graduation or any host of possible reasons, consider using someone in your family as an address to ensure important documents get to you without interruption. Here is a quick example:

My Name Here

---

111 Elm Rd. My City, SC 29588 | 999-999-9999 | Myemail@myuniversity.edu | www.linkedin.com/in/myprofile

2. Education/Objective

To add or delete a job objective is a great debate in most college career offices. There are many opinions on this topic, but let me give you my advice based on my own hiring with both interns and new graduates at top companies like Amazon and other Fortune 500 companies during my three-decade career.

When you are applying for an internship, it is perfectly fine and recommended that you include an objective on your resume right after your contact info and before your education section. Why?

Simple, you want to be clear you are seeking an internship and not a full-time position. When using an objective on your resume, the biggest mistake I see students making is making the objective solely about what they want. With your objective, you want to make sure you demonstrate and understand you are not just seeking job experience, but you want to make a positive contribution to the organization by helping the organization achieve its goals and objectives.

When applying for your first job after graduation, I recommend you lose the objective from your resume unless you are absolutely fixed on that one dream position. The reality is most companies have many different roles and needs that are not advertised. When you are applying for a specific position, the human resource department already knows that you are interested in the position you applied for, or you would not have applied for it in the first place. When they forward your resume to different hiring managers, an objective that is different than the role someone might think you're a great fit for will likely eliminate you from consideration.

Why? One of the biggest fears hiring managers have with new graduates is that they will just take any position to gain experience and then use that experience to land a job more aligned with what they really want to do. As such, hiring managers are looking for clues to see if you are an experience seeker or career seeker. So unless you are dead set on one particular role, lose the career objective. I have seen dozens of times when a manager saw something in someone's resume that aligned with a job, project or need they had that was different than the job the individual was applying for. Put yourself in a position for good things to happen by not using that career or job objective statement.

Now that we have gotten the objective discussion out of the way, we can turn our attention to your education section. First, list your college name and anticipated graduation date. Make sure to list your major and minor if you have one. Also, make sure to include your GPA. You can highlight academic coursework you have completed that is closely related to the position you are applying for. You should include any awards, achievements, or other collegiate success.

Education

University Name, City, State - bachelor's degree - Computer Science - G.P.A.: 3.75 - Planned graduation - December 2023. I am a self-motivated, hardworking senior in the My University's computer science program.

- Founder and President of My University Cybersecurity Club
- Dean's List each year

3. <u>Work Experience</u>

In the experience section, you want to include all your recent work history, whether you believe it is relevant to the job you are applying for or not. Most jobs come with demonstrable skills such as developing your teamwork skills, improving your communication skills, or even dealing with conflict resolution.

In addition to your actual job experiences and internships, there are lots of other types of experiences you might consider adding here. These would include side hustles, freelance work, or charity and volunteer work.

For each position, you want to include the job title, the company name, dates of employment, and outlines of your duties and accomplishments. These can be done in bullet form or in paragraph form. Here is an example below:

Experience

Intern – Company, City, State (Month 202x – Month 202x)

As an intern, I gained experience working to help clients improve the effectiveness of their business and technology. In addition, I supported the help desk by providing technical assistance and support related to computer systems, hardware, software, and password management.

Student Mentor – College, City, State (Summer 202x & 202x)

As a student mentor, provide guidance, motivation, emotional support, and role modeling. Help with exploring majors, setting goals, and identifying clubs and resources of interest.

Team Member – Chick-fil-A City, State (Summer 202x)

As a Chick-fil-A team member, I was responsible for providing an exceptional dining experience for everyone we served each day. Specific duties include greeting customers, taking customer orders, completing transactions on the cash register, operating the drive-thru window, unloading deliveries, and maintaining a clean store environment. I was also responsible for interior designing and planning birthday parties and special events.

4. <u>Key Skills</u>

In this section, you want to list any technical or soft skills that are well-aligned with the job you are applying for. Soft skills are things like communication, teamwork, work ethic, etc. You could also highlight any foreign language skills like "Spanish." If you lived abroad, traveled extensively, or studied abroad, be sure to detail to further highlight your skill.

Skills & Abilities

- CompTIA Security+ certification (Month, 202x)
- Java, HTML & HTML5
- Kali Linux
- Microsoft Office (Excel, Word, PowerPoint, Outlook)
- Licensed Remote Pilot (F.A.A. Part 107 Certified for small, unmanned aircraft systems)
- Strong written and verbal communication skills

5. <u>Activities and associations</u>

Most college students have gained valuable life and work experience skills through both on-campus and off-campus activities and clubs. Sports may have taught you leadership, communication, and teamwork skills. Your Greek life may have done the same. Some clubs may have taught you public speaking, recruiting, and team building. If you held an officer position or led events for a club or association, make sure to make a note of that as well. You can list these as simple bullet points, as I did below, or you can add some details around your responsibilities as we did for our job experience.

Activities & Associations

- Vice President for Delta Sigma Pi
- Treasurer Club Be Your Own Boss
- Member American Management Association

6. Hobbies and interests

This section is optional and can help fill out your resume if you still feel like your resume is too short. You can use this section to bring out your personality and show how you will fit in with the culture of the company you are applying for.

When constructing your resume, it is important to recognize most companies these days use some form of Applicant Tracking System (ATS) to initial screen resumes for consideration. The reality is most companies can't afford to have the human resources needed to initially screen all applicants, so ATS has become a tool most large companies use to initially screen candidates. These systems typically use the underlying job description to write the system algorithms that do the screening. Given this fact, it is extremely important you naturally weave these words the ATS is looking for into your resume. This often will require you to tweak small parts of your resume for each job you apply to. Many students find that just making a few changes to their key skills section based on a particular job description is all that is needed.

Letter of Interest

A letter of interest does not need to be sent via mail. It can be sent via email or even LinkedIn. Letters of interest are effective tools for uncovering those unadvertised positions, and you can send them at any point in your job or internship search. You can use the letter to introduce yourself to a hiring manager in the company in which you want to work.

You should think of a letter of interest as a less formal version of a cover letter you would use when sending in your resume for an advertised position. The key to a well-written letter of interest will highlight why you would be an excellent addition to the company. It should demonstrate your passion, skills, and talents.

Letter of Interest Format:

Company Contact

Use the company's website, press releases, LinkedIn, etc., to identify an individual at your target company to send your letter. I recommend using LinkedIn to establish a relationship and build a warm network. When you have worked on building connections through family or friends, it's likely you are no more than two levels away from your target contact.

Letter Content

The idea is to use your letter to sell yourself. Why would hiring you benefit the company? Why are your values aligned with the company's mission? Have you used the company's products or services for years? In essence, you want to show why the company is of interest to you and why your education, skills, and talents would benefit the company.

Concluding your letter

End your letter by requesting to meet with the employer to discuss possible career opportunities. If you are seeking an internship, you can request an informational interview.

Contact information

Make sure you include your address, phone number, email, and LinkedIn profile. You want to make it easy to be contacted if the company is interested in following up with you.

Elevator Pitch

When attending a networking event, meeting a person in line at Starbucks, or maybe even at a sporting event, you don't typically have a lot of time to tell someone about yourself and your goals and accomplishments. A well-designed elevator pitch will highlight your key skills, talents, and passions. A well-designed elevator pitch will keep individuals engaged and allow you to maximize the time you have.

Part 1 - Determining Your Key Points

1. Initially, you want to focus on a straightforward introduction. This does not mean rattling off a laundry list of your skills and accomplishments. For example, you could say something similar to the following, "Hi, I'm Alan Smith. I just graduated from Coastal Carolina University's marketing program," or, "Hi, I'm Ryan Long, and I am a junior business major at Stanford University."

With simple introductions like the ones above, the person you are speaking with quickly learns your name and where you are in your career journey.

2. Tell them your goals. Now that the person you are speaking with knows who you are and where you went to school, tell them what you are looking for. It might be a job, an

internship, or an informational interview, or a simple LinkedIn connection request.

Let's say you're looking for a job as graduation is approaching, so you are attending a career fair to hopefully get a few leads on a job. You could introduce yourself with something similar to the following, "Hi, I'm Steve Jones. I will graduate in May from Coastal Carolina University with a degree in marketing. I'm seeking a position as a social media coordinator or content writer." The person you are speaking with has learned your name, where you went to school, your major, and what you are looking for, all in two brief sentences.

3. Share your successes. Many people believe the best predictor of future success is past success, so you will want to share your past successes. We don't want to rattle off a list of facts and figures here. Instead, we can frame our response using the context, action, and results (CAR) framework. Using the CAR framework, you will frame your success by giving the context of your accomplishment, the actions taken, and the result you achieved.

   For example, your accomplishment might be that during an internship, you increased the company's sales by 15% in three months. The context of the sales increase was that sales were flat, but you believed by implementing a LinkedIn marketing strategy, sales would grow. The actions you took were to develop a LinkedIn webinar strategy and a follow-up email campaign. Your result was that your company's sales increased by 15%.

4. Share your skill set. You want to communicate the key skills you have that will allow you to make a contribution as part of their team. Many students over-emphasize their hard skills, like their specific degrees, experience, and certifications. Make sure to emphasize your soft skills. Things like your

written and verbal communication skills, leadership, ability to take directions, etc.

For example, you could say something similar to the following, "I have a bachelor's degree in marketing and have worked for two years as a social media manager for a service company. My leaders have always said I have a strong ability to communicate and connect with our clients."

5. We want to end with a strong call to action. Your call to action is designed to take the step in the process after you've made your pitch. This will be different from situation to situation, but it should set up the next step in your relationship with this new contact.

   For example, you could follow up your pitch with something similar to this, "Can we get together next week to talk more? I would love to talk about how I can help your company achieve its goals?" The next step could be a simple request to connect on LinkedIn?" Each conversation will be different. The key is to keep the process moving.

Part 2 - Making Your Speech Engaging

1. It is very important to maintain eye contact with the person whom you are talking with. Don't look past them or down at the floor while speaking with them. Eye contact is critical to making your listener feel connected, and it makes you come across as more professional.

2. You want to be relaxed and confident. It takes some practice to get used to giving your pitch to complete strangers. You likely will be nervous, but if you believe in yourself, it is likely your listener will believe it too.

3. Use powerful and engaging words. Make sure to use your voice tone and cadence to convey energy and enthusiasm.

4. Pay attention to your body language along with that of your listener. Make adjustments based on the verbal and nonverbal feedback you receive. You want to maintain an open and friendly posture. Stand directly in front of your listener, stand up straight, and don't fidget or place your hands in your pocket.

5. Connect with the company's vision and mission. The most compelling elevator pitches are those that connect with the listener and the company's mission. They go beyond the facts and figures and connect at an emotional level.

6. Avoid industry-specific jargon. You can quickly lose your listener's attention if your pitch is filled with jargon and acronyms. You may be speaking to a recruiter who has to recruit for a vast number of different positions and likely will not be well-versed and understand exactly what you're saying if your pitch is loaded with industry jargon and buzzwords. Keep your language simple and engaging, and it will serve you well.

7. Your pitch is the beginning, not the end. You don't want to just smile and walk away at the end of your pitch. You want to engage with your listener. If your listener doesn't have a question for you, make sure to ask your listener questions. What is their role with the company? What do they like most about working at the company? Engaging with your listener makes your pitch part of the conversation, and thus, it won't come across as a speech.

Part 3 - Practicing Your Speech

1. Time yourself. Once you have the key components of your pitch, time yourself speaking out loud as if you were having a conversation. The goal is to have a compelling 30-second

and 60-second version of your pitch. If it takes you longer than 60 seconds, don't speak faster. Speaking too fast during your pitch will make it feel unnatural or canned, and you will lose the listener's interest.

2. Improve your pitch. Once you've spoken your pitch out loud a couple of times, you'll want to continue to improve it. If your pitch is too long, eliminate or streamline parts of your presentation. As you gain new experiences, you will want to update your pitch to reflect your growth, skills or changing goals.

3. Adjust your pitch based on your circumstances. The reason we want to have a 30-second and a 60-second pitch is to allow us to adjust for each situation and adjust it to match the need. If you're at a career fair, for instance, you'll want to focus on landing a job or internship interview.

4. Make your pitch natural. Make sure your pitch doesn't end up sounding rehearsed. You should be well-rehearsed and know what you want to say, but your pitch needs to come off naturally and feel fresh.

5. Get feedback. Once you have your pitch well rehearsed and timed, ask a couple of your friends to provide you with some feedback. Your friends can help you with content, let you know if you seem too rehearsed, and if your pitch is engaging.

Research – Industry, Company, Individuals.

Good preparation will help you perform your best during your interviews. As Ben Franklin was fond of saying, by failing to plan, you are preparing to fail.

Industry Research

A quick online search will return pages and pages of information about an industry. In addition, virtually any industry will have associations, trade groups, lobbyists, etc., that are great resources for detailed industry information. Many company websites will provide valuable industry information, research, and industry news. And, of course, many third-party consultants conduct industry research and studies.

Regardless of the sources of your research, you want to pay attention to a few key pieces of data.

- Who are the large companies in the industry
- What are the key financial ratios and benchmarks
- Is the industry growing and profitable
- What are the competitor dynamics
- What are the barriers to entry
- What are the major markets and products sold
- External factors impacting the industry

Porter's Five Forces model is a valuable way to evaluate industries as well. The model includes the following:

- The threat of new entrants
- Buying power of customers
- Supplier power

- Threat of substitutes
- Industry competitors

Research can be time-consuming, and you may not always be in a position to spend a lot of time doing research. But you will want to make sure you can answer the following questions:

- Who are the major companies in the industry?
- What trends are driving the industry?
- What are the strengths, weaknesses, opportunities, and threats facing the industry?

Company Research

I recommend you start at the company's website first, as this will give you information about the company's values, mission, and culture. Next, head over to Google and do a search on the company you are interested in. When researching a company, you want to learn about the following:

- Company mission, culture, and values.
- Recent news and events.
- Current customers, suppliers, and partners.
- Strengths, Weaknesses, Opportunities, and Threats (SWOT)

<u>Size and Growth Patterns</u>

Understanding the size of a company and the markets it serves provides valuable insights into its future opportunities. Take a look at things like:

- Does the company have international operations?
- Is the company growing or in decline?
- How many different markets does the company serve?
- How many people does the company employ?
- How many customers does the company serve?
- How many divisions or office/production locations does the company have?

Direction and Planning

By reviewing a company's investor presentations, press releases, news articles, and website, you can get a good idea about the company's future plans and priorities. Key areas to focus on are:

- The company's current priorities and projects.
- How aligned is the company's mission statement with your values?
- Who are the company's key customers?
- What major challenges and opportunities are facing the company?
- Where is the company in its product cycle?

Products or Services

Prior to any informational or regular interview, you need to have a working knowledge of the firm's core products and services. You want to be aware of the following:

- The products and services the company offers.
- What markets do the company's products or services serve?
- How does the company position its products and services in the marketplace?
- Does the company follow a strategy of innovation, fast following, low cost, etc.?

Competitive Profile

Is the company a leader in its industry? Companies ranked number one or two in their industry typically grow faster and provide more career advancement opportunities.

- What are the company's core products?
- Who are the major competitors in the industry?
- What weaknesses does the company have to overcome?
- What are some of the company's major achievements?
- How will technology impact the future of the company and industry?
- Is the company a technology leader or a laggard?

Culture and Reputation

Culture and reputation are often open to interpretation. But you can learn a lot about a company through its actions:

- Does the company have a history of laying off employees?
- What's the company's merger and acquisition strategy?
- What is the company's mission?
- What is the company's reputation in the industry?
- Does the company have a bureaucratic management structure?
- Does the company provide world-class benefits to employees?

Company History

The future often is shaped by the past. Looking at the company's history can give you some insights into how it may perform in the future. A few things to consider include the following:

- When was the company founded?
- Is the company publically traded or privately owned?
- How many different subsidiaries or divisions?
- How has the company's product and services changed over time?
- What is the company's annual growth rate?

Company Financials

Understanding the financial well-being of a company is a critical component of your career search. The stronger a company's finances, the better positioned it is to invest in the future and weather the ups and downs of the business cycle. Some key things to consider are:

- What are the trends in the company's sales?
- What are the company's earnings trends?
- What is the company's market capitalization?
- How sound is the company financially?
- Are profits trending up or down?

- What is the company's revenue per employee?
- What is the company's debt-to-equity ratio?

Individual Research

Start by researching the company's website and identifying the company's leaders. Most firms have an about us page or a meet the team page where the key members of the team are highlighted. Next, head over to LinkedIn and review the profiles of the company's leaders. Always make sure to review the LinkedIn profiles of anyone you will interview or will be reaching out to for interviewing. Make a special note of any interests, groups, or volunteer activities highlighted. Pay attention to their individual background and career progression. Take a look at any posts they may have made on LinkedIn, as this is an indication of areas important or meaningful to them. Ultimately, beyond gaining insights into the individual you will be talking with, you are looking for areas of common interest. Anything from their hometown, college, hobbies, etc., are all great areas you can use to connect.

Preparation – Modality, Questions, Flow.

It is important to pick questions that are aligned toward filling in your knowledge gap in your target career field. It is also important to factor in where you are in the decision-making process. Maybe you have not selected a specific major yet. In that case, you would want to lean into questions that would help you with that decision. Maybe you have selected a major, but you are unsure what specific career track within that major is right for you. Regardless of your situation, take the time to plan the interview and ask questions that will create the most value for you. You want to focus on topics around the nature of a person's work, how someone can get started in the field and effective methods for breaking into the industry.

In a typical twenty or thirty-minute interview, you may only have time to ask 5-7 questions, so select ones that align with your curiosity and future goals. Use some of the following questions or develop some questions yourself.

- What are your key responsibilities as a...?
- What does a typical day (or week) look like for you?
- What things do you like most about your job?
- What things do you not enjoy about your job?
- What kind of challenges do you face on a daily basis?
- What are some of the typical decisions you have to make in your role?
- How does your role work with other parts of the organization?
- How does your job affect your lifestyle?
- What changes do you think will likely influence the industry in the coming years?
- What are some of the typical career paths in this industry?
- What kinds of academic or service accomplishments tend to be valued for entry-level positions?
- What other careers would you recommend I consider for my future?
- What interested you in this career or industry?
- How did you start your career?
- What are a few entry-level jobs that would provide good career experience?
- What advice would you have for me as I work toward launching my career?
- Did your college major help you in your career?
- To reach the top of the field, are there any special education or training requirements?
- What skills and attributes do successful people in this industry/position possess?
- What was the background of the people you recently hired out of college?
- What are some paths students can take to find a position in this industry?
- Could you recommend any websites, blogs, trade journals, or trade associations that would help prepare me for my career?

- If you had the opportunity to start your career over, what things would you do differently?
- What insights or advice would you give a college student looking to enter the field?
- Could you recommend anyone else I could speak with to gain more information?

The Three Phases – Introduction and Small Talk, Q&A, and Closing.

<u>Introduction & Small Talk</u>

Make sure you come across enthusiastically and appreciative. Make sure to thank the person for taking the time to meet with you. And make sure to ask how their day is going.

"I want to thank you for taking the time to meet with me today." If someone you know set up the meeting, make sure to mention that: "I was very excited when _____ said you would be willing to meet with me!

Be prepared to give your elevator pitch, as most people will want to learn a little about you before jumping right into a career discussion. You want to be ready to direct the interview as this is an informational interview, so you should be prepared to control the process. Try to create a natural conversation, but you should allow your interviewee to do most of the talking.

<u>Question & Answers</u>

You really want to spend some time preparing a list of questions that will provide insight into the daily activities and interactions involved in the position and industry you have an interest. The person you are interviewing is living the business every day; they can provide you the insights you just can't get from the classroom. The information you receive may confirm or change your interest in the field. I had one student who loved to travel, so it seemed natural for her to pursue a tourism degree. During her informational interviews, she learned about shift work, holiday work, and long hours. She learned that she would have little time to travel with her friends and family. The insights she gained during her informational interviews put her on a different career path.

The knowledge you gain during your informational interviews will allow you to gain more detailed knowledge and will allow you to make better career decisions. Make sure to respect the interviewer's time and stick to the timeframe that was established for the interview.

Follow up – Post Interview, Regular Cadence.

You always want to show your appreciation by sending a thank you email or note card. I recommend sending a thank you 24 hours after the informational interview and no longer than 48 hours. If you send the note too quickly, it seems like an obligatory gesture. Wait too long, and it seems like an attempt to correct a big oversight. By waiting 24 hours, you will have a chance to reflect on your conversation and respond in a thoughtful manner. You not only want to thank them for their time but make sure to highlight one or two things that you found really helpful.

Following up is not a one-time thing. You should establish a regular cadence to update your contacts by providing updates on your coursework, research, and other activities and progress. You can also share industry articles or stories you think may be relevant and helpful. By meeting with you, they have started the process of becoming vested in your success. You want to make sure you continue to build and foster that relationship.

While the informational interview is not about landing a job at the moment, many students find that the process of the informational interview does lead them to a position. And even if the interview doesn't lead directly to a job, the knowledge and information gained during the process will prepare you well for future success.

Internships

Internships are critical to your success in quickly finding a job at graduation. The National Association of Colleges and Employers (NACE) reviewed the results for over a half million four-year college graduates. They looked at over 300 colleges and discovered that just a fraction, over 50%, had landed a full-time job within six months of graduation.

Students with internship experience are 35% more likely to get a job offer after graduating than those students with no internships. So, researching college internship programs is very critical to your future success. Let's look at a few big benefits you gain when working an internship:

1. Practical experience.

You would be hard-pressed to find an employer who would say a candidate's experience did not play a factor in their decision to hire a candidate. When you gain internship experience, you gain practical experience. This experience gives you a competitive advantage over other students who have not landed an internship. Remember, students with internship experience are 35% more likely to have at least one job offer after graduating.

2. Internships are dress rehearsals.

Many employers use internships as a dress rehearsal, choosing to hire students upon graduation who shined during their internship. Internships serve as the "primary source that large companies use to recruit their full-time employees," according to Joshua Kahn, assistant director of research and public policy for NACE. That makes a lot of sense if you think about it. Interns not only gain practical experience but build direct relationships and develop a deep understanding of the company's culture. Interns get an opportunity to demonstrate they are quick learners, can take direction, and fit in with the team.

3. <u>You likely will be paid more upon graduation.</u>

Data compiled by the Economic Policy Institute showed that students with paid internship experience received median offers some 30% above those for students with no paid internship. The relationship held true across the for-profit and non-profit sectors. While the relationship held true in the government sector as well, the gap was smaller at 14.7%.

4. <u>You likely will earn college credit.</u>

Most colleges provide credit toward your degree for participating in qualified internships. Typically, this requires a company to fill out some paperwork with your college's career services office and then provide some status updates on your performance. Most colleges require you to get your internship preapproved prior to you starting, so make sure you check with your advisor to ensure the proper protocols are followed.

5. <u>Internships bridge the gap between your perception and reality.</u>

Many students find there is a big gap between their coursework and the work they will actually be doing in their field. I have had students who were Resort and Tourism majors and who found out they hated the shift work in the field. I have Marketing majors find out they did not like the analytics side of marketing but loved the event planning side. I have had accounting students discover they hated sitting behind a desk eight to twelve hours a day, entering the same tax numbers into the same spreadsheets day after day but loved wealth management. Internships typically allow you to test drive a wide variety of activities and can really help you find clarity in your future career desires.

6. <u>You'll learn how your field interacts with others.</u>

In college, most of your coursework is done in a vacuum. In the real world, it is the exact opposite. You will be working with clients, support departments, vendors, partners, and a whole host of other stakeholders. Learning how your work interacts with and supports other stakeholders helps you develop a deeper understanding of how you will be applying your in-class lessons in the real world. You will also likely develop gaps in your skill sets and be able to develop a plan to close those gaps.

7. You'll build your confidence.

The more experience you gain, the more confidence you will develop. With a higher level of confidence, you will interview better and be more relaxed when you do start your career. Transitioning from college to the work world can be stressful, but extra confidence can go a long way in making that transition quite a bit easier.

8. You'll build your network.

During your internship, you should not only be focused on gaining experience and doing great work but on building your network. Everyone you work with, and meet is someone you can potentially connect with on LinkedIn. You also want to nurture and develop as many personal relationships as possible. Developing a network of mentors who can guide you along as you move toward graduating and starting your career is invaluable.

9. You will gain an edge over the bots.

Most large companies today use what is called an applicant tracking system (ATS) to screen candidate resumes. When you gain internship experience, you gain valuable skills to include on your resume and LinkedIn profile. Most of the bots (computer screening algorithms) use the underlying job description to screen candidates. When your skills align better with the job description, your odds of getting the opportunity for a job interview increase significantly.

10. You'll make some real cash.

Most internships these days pay really well. In fact, the average wage for interns was $20.76 per hour based on a survey of 267 large employers during the summer of 2020. Over half of those companies helped interns with $2,500 for housing and $1,700 for travel expenses.

Volunteering

Volunteering can be a great substitute and addition to any actual internship work. Charities have the same needs as for-profit businesses, and they always seem to need help with everything from marketing to event organization to, well, you name it. Most recruiters surveyed placed volunteer experience on par with work experience. According to a recent Deloitte survey:

- 92% believe volunteering expands an employee's professional skills.
- 85% are willing to overlook resume shortfalls when an employee includes volunteering on a resume.
- 82% of recruiters are more likely to choose a candidate with volunteering experience.
- 80% believe volunteering is an effective way to boost leadership skills.
- 73% believe people who volunteer are more successful.

Not only is volunteering great for gaining practical skills to improve your skills, but it is also a great way to gain insight into your future career work. The idea is to continually try things that will give you new experiences. You won't find your passion sitting on your couch playing Fortnite with all your free time. So, get out there and keep trying new things!

Filling In The Gap

No matter how well-organized your college major is, there will likely be gaps between your education, experience, and dream job. Take a look at online sites like Indeed.com and LinkedIn.com and identify eight to ten jobs that you would love to have after graduation.

Once you identify those eight to ten positions, review the position requirements, and make a list of the skill sets and requirements for each of those positions. You will likely notice a large overlap in the skills employers are looking for in those positions. Now you want to rate yourself on a scale of zero to ten on how well you meet each individual skill or requirement. A rating of zero means you don't possess that skill at all, and a rating of ten means you perfectly match or exceed the needed skill or requirement.

After you have completed this initial gap analysis, you want to look at your remaining coursework. Look at each class in your course catalog and identify which skills you will gain through your coursework as you move toward graduation. Create a column on your spreadsheet labeled "plan to fill the gap" and add a note that you will fill the gap through your coursework.

Now I want you to identify the gaps that still remain between you and your dream job. You want to create a plan to fill those gaps before graduation. For each gap, ask yourself if you can fill the gap with an elective course, an internship, a volunteer position, an online training, or certification course, etc. The key is to fill as many gaps as possible before graduation. Once all your gaps are filled, work on moving all your skills toward a rating of ten. Make sure you realize that not all skills listed in a job description are core skills. If you see the same skill being required across many of your selected job descriptions, you can bet that it is a core skill you will need.

Keep in mind things are rapidly changing in the world, so make sure at least once a year you repeat this exercise to ensure your gap analysis is current and updated with any new skill sets that might have emerged in your dream job.

Campus Resources

Despite the high value offered by most college career resource centers, they are typically under-utilized by students. Studies by the Gallup organization have shown that students that utilize campus career resource centers are more likely to find a full-time job upon graduation (67% vs. 59%). Not only are students more likely to find a job, but they are also more likely to find a job that is fulfilling.

Even with these impressive numbers on their side, only about half of college students utilize their college's career services. As career centers are not placement firms and they don't typically job search for you, students often don't see the value in working with their college career services.

Career services on campuses typically focus on career planning and exploration. They can help you prepare your resume, prepare effective cover letters, and assist you in preparing for interviews. They can help you find a career that is aligned with your interests and talents. They can help ensure you put your best foot forward in each step of the job search process.

You want to utilize all available resources at your disposal to gain an edge over other students competing for the same positions. Your college career center should be an integral part of your career planning.

Mentorship, AKA Your Personal Board of Directors

The clearer your goals come into focus, the more successful your mentorship relationship will be. If you are looking for help identifying your career goals, you will benefit from a different set of mentors than someone who is laser-focused on what they want to do.

No matter where you are in your life's journey, the first step is identifying where you want to go with your mentor relationship prior to engaging with potential mentors. Many students make the mistake of seeking a mentor who is uber-successful in their career. While this can be beneficial, it also can be limiting.

I want you to take a broader view of mentorship. I want you to think of your mentors as your personal board of directors. Just like businesses have a diverse board of directors to keep them on track, you should assemble a diverse board of directors to serve as your mentors and keep your career and life on track. A great place to look for mentors to assemble your board would be upperclassmen, professors, alumni, internships, and your professional and personal networks.

Connect With Upperclassmen

One of the most often overlooked and effective mentors are the juniors and seniors all around you. They have experienced the struggle to pick a major, find internships, and navigate their future careers.

They don't have all the answers, but they have recent, timely experience on the path you are currently on. They are in a position to help you connect with other students, clubs, associations, and resources that can help you on your journey. They can help you cut through the seemingly endless maze of campus resources. They also aren't out of touch or face generational bias that may impact their ability to connect with you and your individual situation.

One of the most effective tools I have found to communicate important messages in the classroom is to bring in upperclassmen who learned the lessons the hard way. Let's face it, sometimes we are much more open to a message when it comes from one of our peers.

Connect With Your Professors

Building relationships with your professors can benefit you in many ways, both inside and outside the classroom. Alumni routinely reach out to their professors for internship recommendations. I have lost count of the number of students who landed amazing jobs as a result of a professor's recommendation. Recommendations for graduate school will typically require a couple letters of recommendation from faculty in your program. Special scholarships, research, awards, and other department opportunities can stem directly from your relationship with your professors.

As a business school professor, for example, I have contacts in the industry that can help my students potentially land a competitive internship or interview. An art history professor could likely recommend you for that coveted museum position. A psychology professor could assign you to their research project. Regardless of your field of study, the vast majority of professors maintain relationships with people in their field, people who can help you with your future career.

To access all these potential benefits, you will need to stand out from other students and put the work into building and maintaining the relationship. Participate in class lectures and discussions and visit your professors during their office hours. Check-in each semester even after you have long taken their class. You want to nurture the relationship long before you seek their assistance with your career. Professors can only call in favors so often. They have to be very selective when they do. You want to make it an easy decision for them to want to help you.

Connect With Alumni

One of the best sources of mentors is your universities alumni network. These folks were once where you are now, and the successful ones love to give back. They love helping others along their path. Heck, the very reason I got into teaching was my desire to help accelerate the success journey for my students. Once you reach a certain financial level of success, the money doesn't drive you anymore. What drives you then, you ask. Impact! A sense of purpose! Purpose is happiness.

Most university career centers have some form of mentorship program. Others maintain an online database of alumni willing to offer guidance. One of the best sources may be LinkedIn. Using the alumni tool on LinkedIn, you gain a large list of potential connections and mentors.

When reaching out to alumni from your school, it is important to come across as looking for a job. You want to use the tools we discussed in the informational interview section of this book. You want to reach out for advice with a clear and simple message. Something along the lines of:

Hi, my name is Amanda Smith, and I'm a 2nd year marketing major at Coastal Carolina University. I found your profile on LinkedIn and was very impressed with your career progression. I would love to get together for 20 minutes for coffee and learn first-hand what it's like to work in the industry.

Connect With Your Internship Colleagues

During your internship, you not only want to learn but build your connections. There are two types of colleagues you want to pay close attention to building connections with. The first is the recent graduates just a year or two into their careers. They are still familiar with the entry-level hiring process and the type of things you will be doing on a daily basis. Next, you want to connect with those managers that have hiring authority. They understand the department's goals, budgets, and future needs of their departments.

Students often connect easily with those employees who are just a few years older than they are, but they can struggle to connect with managers. Use your informational interview questions as a bridge to connect with the more senior leaders in the organization. As you build these relationships, you want to make sure you continue to stay in contact and further develop your relationships long after your internship ends.

Reciprocate With Your Connections

The mentor-mentee relationship is not a one-way street. Way too often, students shine light on their needs and forget that the most effective relationship is actually like a two-way street. Put simply, you should look to contribute value whenever you can. Can you do your mentor a favor? Can you teach them about a new app that will make their job easier? Can you gather some competitor intelligence to help them gain an edge? The key is to find ways to add value, and you will get much more out of your relationships.

Conclusion

A fulfilling life is one without regrets. You have worked hard, but you have also enjoyed the journey. You have done what you love and loved what you do. This is possible when you understand your purpose and live a life that aligns with it.

Your purpose is more than a career path or profession. It is the reason why you exist in this world. It's your unique set of talents, passions, and values that shape who you are and how you contribute to society. By understanding your purpose, you are able to better direct your life choices towards meaningful work, relationships, and activities that make you happy and bring joy to others.

Purpose-driven lives are also more resilient and adaptive. When life throws curveballs, purpose gives you the strength and direction to pivot and find new ways of achieving your goals. It keeps you motivated when the going gets tough, because purpose is a source of inner power that comes from within.

Purpose is the reason why you do something. It gives you a sense of direction and clarity in life, allowing you to make decisions that are aligned with your values and goals. Without understanding your purpose, it's easy to become lost in the day-to-day grind without achieving any real fulfillment from life. Finding your purpose requires taking a step back to reflect on what you believe in and where you want to go.

Understanding your purpose is the key to a fulfilling life, as it allows you to do work that inspires you and makes this world a better place. By taking the time to understand yourself, your talents, passions, and values, you can set goals that will lead to a more meaningful and satisfying life. Purpose holds the power of true fulfillment - if we tap into it, we can create lives full of joy and impact.

The conclusion is clear: discovering your purpose is a critical step in creating a fulfilling life. Through understanding ourselves and our unique gifts, we can use our talents in ways that make us truly happy while also making a positive contribution to the world. Purpose is not just a vague concept - it's something that can be found and utilized to create a life of meaning and fulfillment. So take the time to get to know yourself, your unique purpose, and start creating a journey towards an extraordinary life.

Notes

1. Transfer & Mobility - 2015 - National Student Clearinghouse Research Center (nscresearchcenter.org)
2. 10 Shocking Workplace Stats You Need To Know (forbes.com)
3. Global Research: See the World in Data | Gallup
4. How your salary and the way you spend money affect your happiness (cnbc.com)
5. New Study Shows That More Money Buys More Happiness, Even For The Rich (forbes.com)
6. https://hbr.org/2018/11/9-out-of-10-people-are-willing-to-earn-less-money-to-do-more-meaningful-work
7. https://www.inc.com/salesforce/revops-centers-finance-and-sales-around-the-customer-driving-growth.html
8. https://www.eehealth.org/blog/2019/12/life-purpose/#:~:text=It%20can%20propel%20you%20to,a%20clear%20sense%20of%20purpose.
9. https://intellihr.com/en-us/insights/goal-setting-and-tracking
10. Latest Research on Meaning and Purpose At Work (betterup.com)
11. Why Volunteering Is The Single Most Overlooked Skill On Resumes (fastcompany.com)
12. Deloitte Volunteer IMPACT Research | Deloitte US
13. https://www.petersons.com/blog/malcolm-gladwells-david-and-goliath-and-your-college-decision/
14. https://www.businessinsider.com/malcolm-gladwells-david-and-goliath-2013-10
15. Estimated Class Sizes: More Than 90 National Universities - Public University Honors
16. Why colleges' "average class size" statistics are misleading — and how to fix them | by Kyle Giddon | Medium
17. The Impact of Distance from Home on Student-Athlete's GPA at Northwestern College Misael Bruzzone and Hailey Louw https://nwcommons.nwciowa.edu/cgi/viewcontent.cgi?article=1095&context=celebrationofresearch
18. College Sizes: Small, Medium, or Large? | College Data

19. Bigger High Schools Seem to Be Better - Los Angeles Times (latimes.com)
20. Data Point—Beginning College Students Who Change Their Majors Within 3 Years of Enrollment (ed.gov)
21. How Much Does College Cost? | College Data
22. The College Mental Health Crisis: A Call for Cultural Change - Part 2 - MGH Clay Center for Young Healthy Minds
23. Press Release - A Majority of College Students with Disabilities Do Not Inform School, New NCES Data Show - April 26, 2022 (ed.gov)
24. Students with Disabilities – PNPI
25. 50% of the Class of 2020 got full-time jobs 6 months after graduation (cnbc.com)
26. https://www.bold.com/transformation-in-the-workplace/sound-investment-or-money-down-the-drain-experts-weigh-in-on-the-real-value-of-a-bachelors-degree/#:~:text=According%20to%20a%20recent%20CareerBuilder,positions%20hadn't%20necessarily%20evolved.
27. Networking Statistics Everyone Should Know (2022) (apollotechnical.com)
28. 73+ Surprising Networking Statistics to Boost Your Career (review42.com)
29. 9 Worthwhile Scholarship Websites And Search Engines – Forbes Advisor
30. Do college internships lead to jobs? Yes, especially if internships are paid. (ajc.com)
31. Paid internship wages are the highest they've ever been (cnbc.com)
32. How to Use Career Centers to Advance Your Career (learnhowtobecome.org)
33. Booklet_Template_2016 (luminafoundation.org) Great Jobs. Great Lives. The Value of Career Services, Inclusive Experiences, and Mentorship for College Graduates.
34. *Berkeley University of California* *https://career.berkeley.edu/Info/InfoQuestions*

Made in the USA
Las Vegas, NV
16 May 2026

47152283R00115